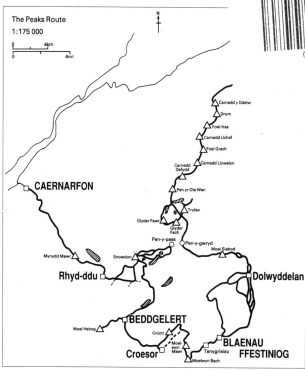

The Peaks Route
1:175 000

0 — 4km
0 — 4ml

Carnedd y Ddelw
Drum
Foel-fras
Carnedd Uchaf
Foel Grach
Carnedd Llywelyn
Carnedd Dafydd
Pen yr Ole Wen
Tryfan
Glyder Fawr
Glyder Fach
Pen-y-pass
Pen-y-gwryd
Moel Siabod
Mynydd Mawr
Snowdon
Rhyd-ddu
Dolwyddelan
CAERNARFON
Moel Hebog
Cnicht
Moel-wyn Mawr
Tanygrisiau
BLAENAU FFESTINIOG
BEDDGELERT
Croesor
Moelwyn Bach

The climb from
Llyn Ogwen
to the
Carneddau Ridge
via
Pen yr Ole Wen.

inside front cover:
Yr Wyddfa
in winter snow
from
Llyn Llydaw.

inside back cover:
WALK SNOWDONIA
series
front covers.

back cover:
The Glyders
from above
Capel Curig.

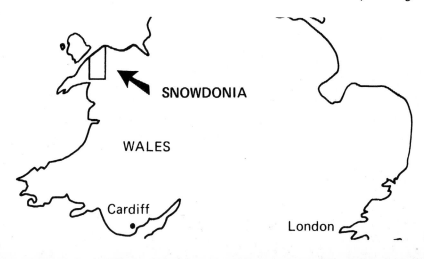

SNOWDONIA

WALES

Cardiff

London

By the same author

	ISBN
Walk in the beautiful Conwy Valley	1–872050–00–X
Walk in magnificent Snowdonia	1–872050–02–6
Walk Snowdonia ancient trackways Roman roads packhorse trails	1–872050–03–4
Walk in the Romantic Vale of Ffestiniog Porthmadog Cricieth	1–872050–04–2

Available through bookshops and other bookseller outlets

All are displayed on the inside back cover

Ralph Maddern

Walk
Snowdonia
PEAKS

to Sam Joe Robert

Focus Publications Ltd

© Ralph Maddern

First published in Great Britain 1988
Revised and re-published 1993

Focus Publications Ltd
9 Priors Road
Windsor
Berkshire SL4 4PD

ISBN: 1–872050–05–0

Printed in Great Britain by
Grosvenor Press (Portsmouth) Ltd.

Walk Snowdonia Peaks

Order of Ascent

Mynydd Mawr
Snowdon
Moel Hebog

Cnicht
Moelwyn Mawr
Moelwyn Bach

Moel Siabod
Tryfan
Glyder Fach
Glyder Fawr

Pen yr Ole Wen
Carnedd Dafydd
Carnedd Llywelyn
Foel Grach
Carnedd Uchaf
Foel-fras
Drum
Carnedd y Ddelw
Tal y Fan
Conwy Mountain

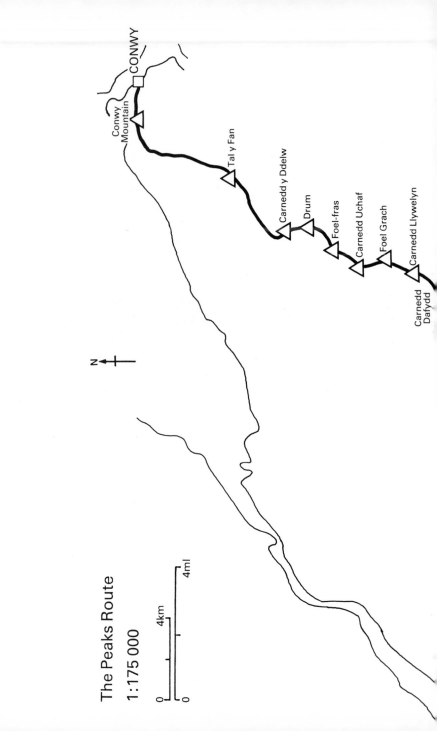

The Peaks Route
1:175 000

0   4km
0   4ml

N

CONWY

Conwy Mountain

Tal y Fan

Carnedd y Ddelw

Drum

Foel-fras

Carnedd Uchaf

Foel Grach

Carnedd Llywelyn

Carnedd Dafydd

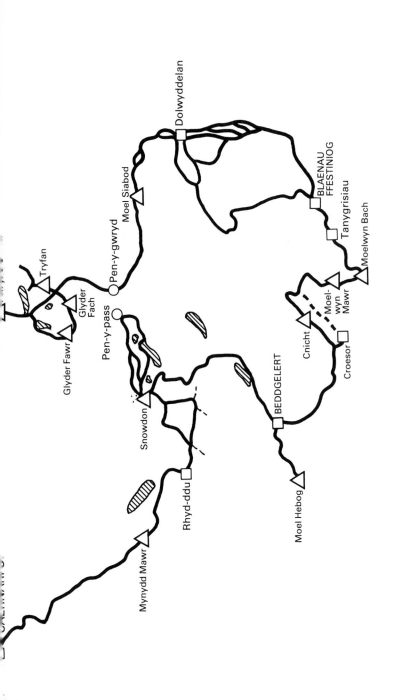

Contents

The Peaks in Perspective

Contents

Compass Bearings

Pedometer Readings

and the Peaks

Accuracy of position and direction is ensured by combining two kinds of measurement: distance registered by a pedometer, and direction recorded by a compass.

A pedometer reading may be taken to be correct to the nearest one-tenth of a kilometre or one hundred metres: 1.7km is within the range 1.65km to 1.75km, 1650 metres to 1750 metres.

A compass bearing of 080° can be accepted as lying within the arc 075° to 085°.

To determine a bearing, hold a hand compass in a horizontal position and allow the needle to steady. Turn the circle graduated in degrees until the N/S marking – 0°/360° to 180° – lies exactly beneath the needle.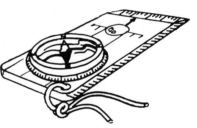

If a bearing in this text is to be followed move the base platform until its centre line registers the required reading on the graduated circle.

If the bearing of an object from a position on the ground is required, move the base platform until its centre-line is aligned with the object. Read the object's bearing on the graduated circle.

If seeking a bearing from an Ordnance Survey map in order to follow a direction on the ground,

★ place the centre of the graduated circle on the map position from which the bearing is to be taken

★ move the grid lines of the graduated circle to coincide with those of the OS map

★ Align the base platform's centreline on the map with the object whose bearing is required and read the bearing on the graduated circle.

Welsh

Place names in Wales are fascinating because of the descriptions they offer of their locations. That is why interpretations are given where this is possible. Understanding what the name means is often a major clue to knowing the place itself. Pronunciation can be quite difficult for a non-Welsh speaker but it is worth trying to get the right sound. The main sounds, where these differ from English, are set out below.

a   as in *are*
c   always hard as in *car*
Ch   as in the Scottish *loch*
e   'ay' as in *say*
f   as in the English '*v*'
Ff   as in the English '*f*'
g   always hard as in *give*
Ll   place the tongue to form 'l' but emit a passage of air through the tongue to merge with the following letter
r   rolled more strongly than in English
Rh   both the 'r' and the 'h' are pronounced
Th   as in *both*
Dd   also 'th' but as in *this*
u   'i' as in *it* or 'ee' as in *feet*
w   'oo' as in roost (Llanrwst = Llanroost) – it also works like the English 'w'
y   'u' as in *fun* or 'ee' as in *feet* or 'i' as in *pin* (you have to listen)

J, K, Q, V, X and Z do not appear in Welsh as these sounds are conveyed by other letters or diphthongs.

As with some Welsh poetry the evocative quality in the term *critch-cratch* eludes adequate representation in English. *Critch-cratch* refers to a gate hung in a U or V-shaped enclosure and is, therefore, impassable to stock animals. It is sometimes known as a 'kissing gate'.

Critch-cratch seems much more illustrative and evocative.

Countryside COMMISSION

Walking the Snowdonia Peaks of Eryri is a deservedly popular activity which, however, can lead to over-use and consequent erosion in some areas.

The use of alternative new routes, if not properly planned, may result in further erosion and disturbance or damage to plants and animals.

In seeking to safeguard the unique character of Eryri, a range of measures need to be employed, including:

* careful selection of alternative routes where possible

* sensitive work to improve path surfaces

* reduction of grazing, where practicable, to increase the resistance of vegetation to wear.

Walkers are asked to co-operate by using good existing tracks where these are available and avoiding over-used areas.

 COUNTRYSIDE COUNCIL FOR WALES

COMISIWN Cefn Gwlad

Mae cerdded llwybrau Eryri yn weithgaredd poblogaidd, a theg hynny. Ond fe all arwain at eu gorddefnyddio ac erydu'r tir yn y mannau mwyaf poblogaidd.

Fe ellid defnyddio llwybrau eraill ond fe allai hynny, heb gynllunio gofalus, arwain at erydu pellach a niweidio planhigion ac anifeiliaid.

Er mwyn diogelu cymeriad unigryw Eryri bydd rhaid dibynnu ar amrywiaeth o atebion gan gynnwys:

* dewisiad gofalus o lwybrau eraill lle mae'n bosibl

* gwaith sensitif i wella'r llwybrau presennol

* cyfyngu ar y pori, lle bo hynny'n ymarferol, er mwyn i'r llystyfiant fedru gwrthsefyll y traul yn well.

Gofynnir am gydweithrediad y cerddwyr, trwy ddefnyddio'r llwybrau da yn unig ac osgoi y rhandiroedd sydd wedi eu gor-ddefnyddio.

CYNGOR
CEFN GWLAD
CYMRU

The Peaks in Perspective

May we begin at sea?

The sea has always set the stage for the drama of mountains, so it would be appropriate to begin offshore. We might choose a yacht; but if one should not be available, the voyage may as easily be made in the imagination.

A suitable point of embarkation would be *Ynys Seiriol* – Puffin Island. Set a compass bearing of SW by S into the mouth of the beautiful strait, and across the route once used by Irish raiders on plundering expeditions to this western extremity of the Roman Empire.

Rich pickings could be gathered from these strangers but operations became increasingly hazardous. The defenders had an early warning system triggered by hilltop lookouts signalling to boats moored in coves along the shores. The raiders could be intercepted at sea, establishing a precedent for defending an island against invasion. The Romans were not in need of slaves as there was plenty of indigenous labour available to assist with arterial road construction and any other odd jobs. Therefore, the raiders taken alive were bound back to back, taken out to sea and dumped.

A millenium later the Norman English were unable to conquer overland as the Romans did because the defensive potential of Eryri had become appreciated through local battles for control of Gwynedd. By 1094, Gruffydd ap Cynan (1055-1137) had established himself as king. In November the following year, the Norman English king, William Rufus, advanced into North Wales intending to complete a conquest before the winter. Most of Wales rose in support of Gruffydd who harried Rufus with guerrilla warfare in the mountainous terrain, fought a decisive battle against the invaders at Tomen-y-mur, near Ffestiniog, and followed them in retreat to Chester. The mountain stronghold had enabled the Welsh to secure their independence, but command of the sea was not appreciated as the other vital strategic factor in the power struggle.

Two centuries later, Edward the First's army pressed

forward along the coast, taking key estuaries where castles could be built, castles of such design that resistance to attack by frontal assault was guaranteed. A yacht's eye view of Beaumaris Castle illustrates the benefit of being able to supply by sea, enabling consolidation of power which, in time, would be used to conquer the hinterland.

Near the entrance to the strait, the victorious Gruffydd ap Cynan has his monument in Bangor Cathedral built (1120-39) during his reign and named The Cathedral Church of St Deiniol, who founded a monastery here in the sixth century.

Since then Bangor must have been on everyone's transit map though this is not its most compelling distinction now. In our time, incomers seeking re-evaluation choose this location where trends and contradictions can be viewed in detachment, though not in isolation. Propositions distilled here may be transmitted outwards in a process of interaction. This is no peripheral cauldron bubbling away ineffectually on a hilly headland at the entrance to a scenic strait. Here is a confluence of streams contributing to a process of re-thinking that is perceived as a necessary pre-condition for our world to find its future.

Sailing along the strait one becomes aware of a remarkable structure with a significance transcending its location. Thomas Telford's life (1757–1834) spanned an age when beauty, economy, efficiency, durability and simplicity could all co-exist in harmony. A few questions surface. Why is it that with advanced technology now available such co-existence is, apparently, so difficult to achieve? Is one conditioned subjectively to regard creations of the past with affection that one cannot accord to productions of the present? Will objective evaluations of present creations be possible only after a lapse of time – which may be as far into the future as Telford's creation is in the past?

While engaged in debate with the other half of oneself the yacht has glided southwestward and is now abeam of Plas Newydd, an eighteenth-century house chockful of magnificent painting, set in beautiful grounds and woodland and commanding superb views of the strait and mountains.

What is heritage, one asks the other half. Is it important? What is its relevance to life now? A Chinese proverb presents itself: "To forget one's ancestors is to be a brook without a source, a tree without root." As a westernisation of oriental wisdom, would it be in order to substitute heritage for ancestors? After all, Britain may claim a heritage as extensive as China's if we include the entire span of time back to the New Stone Age whose monuments include Eryri's cromlechs and standing stones: the time when the northern end of the Carneddau yielded *graiglwyd*, the hard grey stone that was fashioned into fine tools for felling forests so that grain could be planted.

Which brings us within Caernarfon's magnetic field. Like a magnet, attraction intensifies as one approaches, though its precise nature is tantalisingly obscure. Not the attraction of a great cathedral whose magnetism derives from the beauty of its structure. Beauty is a wonderful force but it is not at the bottom of this wellspring.

Disembarking in pursuit of an answer, one makes straight for the town walls and castle where, enclosed by a feeling of solid eternity, there is surprise in learning of a time – only seven hundred years ago – when no castle or town walls existed. This site was a place of residence for Welsh princes and their court from which they had been accustomed to rule and quarrel amongst themselves for centuries.

Then, in 1283, everything changed with the arrival of King Edward the First and his army. Before their very eyes the Welsh watched these massive walls rising. Enraged, they attacked (1294–5), occupied the site and demolished as much as they could before being driven off. The Welsh counter-attack strengthened the resolve of the conquering power. With enhanced vigour, construction was resumed in June 1295, directed by the single-minded Edward himself. Power: it is certainly illustrated here. Look at the precision of the geometrical construction. A power that knew what it wanted, knew how to get it and proceeded about its business with total self-confidence. What it lacked was an understanding of how the conquerors a thousand years earlier had established their power on this location.

Further up the hill, astride what is now the Beddgelert Road, lay the epicentre of that classical conquest. The Roman purpose was to secure Anglesey as a source of metals and grain. This required a firmly established power over the whole of North Wales through a network of forts and arterial roads. It was accomplished with remarkable ease compared with that of the Norman English whose success was delayed almost two-hundred years due to the defensive use of Eryri by the Welsh.

Viewing the remains of Segontium today, one has an impression of precise concept. These conquerors understood exactly what they sought, and perhaps that suggests a further reason for Gruffydd ap Cynan's defeat of William Rufus. Did Rufus know why he sought conquest and what he wanted to do with this area of Britain? Certainly, Gruffydd was in no doubt why he felt it imperative to defeat Rufus, just as the Romans were clear about their intentions, as was Edward about his. The two conquests were based upon a logical understanding of the purpose of power, as the architecture of each shows.

At the Segontium Museum we have a suitable location from which to begin an exploration of Snowdonia peaks and, possibly, other kinds of discovery as well.

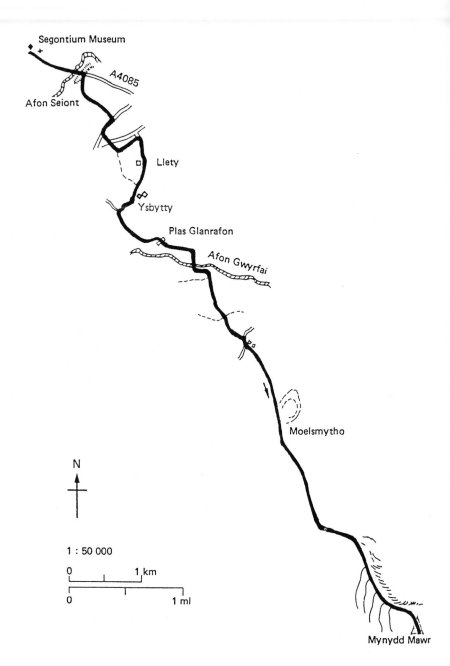

Segontium Museum

A4085

Afon Seiont

Llety

Ysbytty

Plas Glanrafon

Afon Gwyrfai

Moelsmytho

N

1 : 50 000

0   1 km

0   1 ml

Mynydd Mawr

18

Mynydd Mawr

10.9km   6.8ml

From the gate of the museum (0.0km) tread SE along the route of a Roman road, which is now the A4085, to the Parish Church of St Peblig (0.2km). Llanbeblic, the parish which includes the whole of Caernarfon, and this, the Church of Peblig, commemorates a sixth-century saint who chose his site when Segontium would still have been the dominant building on the landscape though the conquerors had departed more than a century following the decline and fall of their empire. That the new era was built upon the ruins of the old appears confirmed by discovery in the church's footings of a Roman altar, now housed in the museum.

After crossing the bridges spanning the Afon Seiont (0.8km) and the track of a dismantled railway, turn right from the road (S) onto a path leading to a wall corner (1.1km). Veer left (SE) across a field to wall steps and a gate (1.3km), cross the next field to a critch-cratch (1.5km), continue to a stile and on to the next critch-cratch and a council road (1.7km). Turn right (SW) to a farm track (1.9km) and left to face a profile of the elephant mountain. In clear weather, the unique shape which Mynydd Mawr presents to the distant eye will ensure we do not lose our objective.

Cross the road (2.1km), follow the track, SE and then NE, to a farm road, and southward to Llety (2.9km). From the stile south of the house continue across a field through two critch-cratches and on, between wall boundaries, to Ysbytty Farm (3.5km). Along the track SW to a farm road (3.7km), turn left (S) and continue southeastward and eastward to Plas Glan-yr-afon (4.5km, 2.8ml).

Suddenly, there is an atmosphere of a different century. Glan-yr-afon is a country house of late-seventeenth, early-eighteenth-century vintage, retaining features with which it was then endowed, including oak panelling, moulded cornices and doorways, tall square chimneys, oil paintings, outbuildings of distinction. All of which may not have endured so well were its location less secluded.

Continue E along a farm track to a track intersection (5.0km). Turn right (S) down to a bridge spanning the sparkling Afon Gwyrfai (5.2km) which is the main supplier of Llyn Cwellyn lying at the eastern foot of Mynydd Mawr. Cross the bridge, turn left to a stile, beyond which a path lies SE up the hill, and E alongside the course of a dismantled railway, once part of a line connecting the area southward to the quarries near Bryngwyn with Caernarfon, Betws Garmon, Rhyd-ddu, Beddgelert and Porthmadog.

The Welsh Highland Railway was a remarkable phenomenon which operated from 1922 to 1937. We shall encounter another part of its heritage south of Beddgelert and take the opportunity to consider efforts being made for its restoration.

Turn right (5.4km) across the old railway track and continue southward past Tan-yr-allt (5.5km) to a track intersection (6.0km). Keeping south-southeastward, follow the path between field walls to a critch-cratch, up the hill past a wall corner to a council road (6.6km).

Southeastward beyond another wall corner (7.2km) there are open spaces at last. Unconstrained by fences or field walls there is a feeling of liberation and urgency to reach the first peak. But first, on the left, are the heathered mounds of Moelsmytho, and on the right, the derelict quarries of Moel Tryfan. Beyond, is a near profile of the mountain which presents its elephant's knee for ascent. We begin on a bearing of about 160°.

Up the line of the ridge there is the rim of the cwm. One imagines suspending from a hang glider in a reckless launch across the precipice, floating above Cwm Du with Cwellyn far below, wheeling northwestward to follow the course of the Afon Gwyrfai, skimming the villages of Betws Garmon and Waunfawr, and on to the towers of Caernarfon Castle. What is there about mountains that stimulates the mind?

Keeping to 160° we find the cairn at Mynydd Mawr's peak (10.9km, 6.8ml; elevation 698m, 2290ft). On a clear day it is a splendid vantage point for viewing a large area of

Eryri. The premier peak itself is enthroned eastward across the valley, attended by its retinue of lesser summits. For the moment we may turn our backs on that court to look through the door – y drws – of the mountain towards the sea and a famous bard's valley: Dyffryn Nantlle.

Robert Williams Parry (1884–1956) won the National Eisteddfod chair at Colwyn Bay in 1910 with a work entitled *Yr Haf* – The Summer. Its theme is love: The Summer of Love, explored with varying emotional associations – exhilaration, pessimism, anticipation, optimism, disappointment, fulfilment – all set within this environment. He was a bard of these mountains, Eryri, which he regarded as a "paradise" and as "a cure for all ills".

The year after his bardic triumph he explained himself in the magazine of the University College of North Wales.

"Quite unmoved by either hope or despair is love's summer. When love and youth walk hand in hand, it is the present that holds undisputed sway. Thus we have three perspectives of summer. First, the passing of summer and its tendency to pessimism; second, the Summer of Love, with its agnostic indifference to the past and future; third, the Evergreen Summer, the summer of the optimist who has learnt the lesson of hope."

Walking over Eryri's peaks we shall have occasion to call upon this bard's thoughts, and others, for illustration or illumination. Meanwhile, what sort of a place in the land of bards gave birth to a bard of enduring renown?

Despite the piles of quarry waste on the valley floor, slate was not Nantlle's first industry. In the seminal period of industrialisation, the eighteenth century, the time when Glan-yr-afon was built, the sunrise industry was copper mining which attracted compulsive Cornishmen. Nantlle was but one spot on the entire earth's surface which received their attentions. They were the most experienced, skilled, persistent and willing travellers to any place worldwide where there was a chance of mining copper. Little evidence remains of the Cornish incomers in Nantlle except for a few names in the parish register. They came, sank shafts, produced copper, and when the ore was worked out they disappeared, presumably to some other copper workings.

Slate workers were altogether different in being a permanent feature of the local scene. The slate industry concentrated Welsh people, Welsh culture and language, into a community that developed a cohesion of its own. All the characteristics of such communities were present here: a common identity based upon language, religion, music, education, tradition. But Dyffryn Nantlle produced something more: bardic brilliance, which is their distinction and our privilege to sample.

Descending SE and E round the rim of Cwm Planwydd there is a view NE to Castell Cidwm, a knoll near the northern end of Llyn Cwellyn, inviting a tantalising question about which side of the lake the Roman road between Segontium and Tomen-y-mur lay. Castell Cidwm could have been a Roman fortification, and a reasonable supposition is that the Castle Cidwm Hotel stands on the site of a Roman residence. Intriguing is the evidence that nature subsumed this piece of ancient civil engineering, as it obliterated from human memory knowledge of Segontium itself which was rediscovered only in the nineteenth century.

Descending to the lower summit, Foel Rudd (12.2km, 7.6ml; elevation 573m, 1878ft), along the boundary of the plantation to the third stile (14.0km), turn NE into the plantation, veer SE to the forestry station, Planwydd (14.9km), and right to Rhyd-ddu (16.0km. 10ml).

A different valley a different world. Or, so it was before the age of instantaneous multi-communication.

Even the Welsh language, though encapsulating a common culture, varied in mode, accent and intonation from

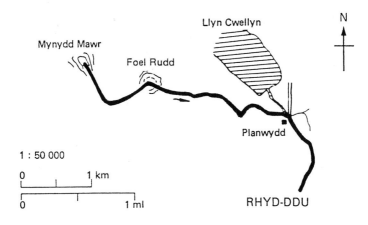

N

Llyn Cwellyn

Mynydd Mawr

Foel Rudd

Planwydd

1 : 50 000

0   1 km

0   1 ml

RHYD-DDU

valley to valley. Occasionally, there were, and are, other unique reasons for clear identification. Dyffryn Nantlle has its bard, Robert Williams Parry. Rhyd-ddu has its bard whose name is a mirror image of Nantlle's. The distinction of Thomas Parry-Williams (1889-1975) is that he won the National Eisteddfod crown and chair in the same year twice – 1912 and 1915. He was a bard of this landscape and liked to be associated with the mountain which this village regards as its own. Being the village closest to Snowdon is satisfying, though the real stimulant to pride, here as in Nantlle, is association with a significant litterateur, who is invisible to the passerby, but for the soul of the community, entirely durable into the future.

The Premier Peak: Yr Wyddfa: Snowdon:

7.5km 4.8ml

From Rhyd-ddu PO (0.0km) walk SE (220°) alongside the A4085 to a lane (0.1km), turn left (E then SE) and continue between two houses to a critch-cratch (0.3km), incidentally bypassing on the right the village school where there is a museum depicting the life and work of Thomas Parry-Williams. The track winds eastward over three stiles to a fourth (2.0km) where there is a fork left to Snowdon, a route we shall take after exploring the one eastward to the base of the mountain's southern spine.

Snowdon is at her most appealing when trailing veils of mist over her loins. Here, she may suddenly reveal her southern foot or expose her dramatic boulders from which gush white water in foaming cascades (3.0km). This is the track used by quarrymen in their daily trek from Rhyd-ddu to the quarry at Snowdon's foot. One has a choice of reaction: to deplore quarry waste as industrial spoilage, or regard it as a special sculpture that time has clothed in rugged beauty. Perhaps, like the Roman road, nature intends to subsume all this evidence of human activity. There are, certainly, indications of such intention. Those bow walls of buildings long deserted: huge rocks, once captured, seek to regain their former resting places. Fern-lined caverns, having yielded their surface overburdens, display mountain streams racing clear-eyed across their floors. Viewing this work of art that consumed the lives of unsung heroes is an experience to replenish the soul before coming to terms with the crags of Yr Wyddfa.

At the top of a slag heap join the track from Beddgelert (4.6km) and continue to a ridge wall where the expanse of Cwm Llan opens, offering a spacious view of Nantgwynant and the lakes Gwynant and Dinas. Our track is northward, up onto the steep ridge and an ever-widening view. To the west there is a broad plain sloping away towards the sea but in the foreground are lakes. Cwellyn (NW), the cradle lake,

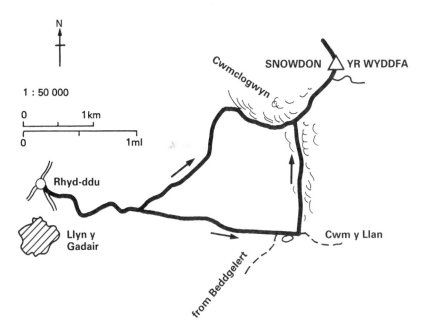

so called because of its shape. To its south lies a smaller shape, Llyn y Gadair (W), less impressive, though a subject chosen by Rhyd-ddu's bard.

i. Ni wêl y teithiwr talog mono bron
     Wrth edrych dros ei fasddwr ar y wlad.
Mae mwy o harddwch ym mynyddoedd hon
     Nag mewn rhyw ddarn o lyn, heb ddim ond bad
Pysgotwr unig, sydd yn chwipio'r dŵr
     A rhwyfo plwc yn awr ac yn y man,
Fel adyn ar gyfeiliorn, neu fel gŵr
     Ar ddyfroedd hunlle 'n methu cyrraedd glan.
Ond mae rhyw ddewin â dieflig hud
     Yn gwneuthur gweld ei wyneb i mi'n nef,
Er nad oes dim gogoniant yn ei bryd,
     Na godidowgrwydd ar ei lannau ef, –
Dim byd ond mawnog a'i boncyffion brau,
Dau glogwyn, a dwy chwarel wedi cau.

25

The jaunty traveller hardly sees it
    Looking across its shallow water at the country.
There is more beauty in her mountains
    Than in a piece of lake, with nothing but the boat
Of a lonely fisherman, who whips water
    Rowing awhile now and then,
Like a wretch in a quandry, or a man
    On the waters of a nightmare unable to reach the
bank.
But there is a magician with a fiendish charm
    Making its surface look to me like heaven,
Although there is no splendour in its complexion,
    Or anything special on its banks, –
Nothing but peat bog and brittle stumps,
Two cliffs, and two quarries which are closed.

One trudges upward – northward on this southern spine, veering to NE on reaching the narrow pass, Bwlch Main, leading to the summit. And here there is the fork where the alternative route meets the ridge path.

From the stile (2.0km) where the path from Rhyd-ddu forks, veer left on a general bearing of 070° up to the rim of Cwmclogwyn, a restless cauldron that is apt to brew up whirling mist and hurl it over Snowdon in vast masses of ubiquitous grey. One might be on a storm-bound ship listening to a pitiless sea discharging its fury at an intruder. Another impression is offered by a bard, Eos Bradwen.

ii.   Eryri fynyddig i mi,
             Bro dawel y delyn yw.

             The mounains of Eryri for me,
             Serene land of the harp.

Suddenly, the tempest relents – in support of the bard, perhaps! – the cwm reveals its ponderous lakes as a curtain raiser to a dramatic landscape extending to the ocean. The cwm's rim demands a zigzagging manoeuvre, easing along the contours then crossing them to join the southern ridge route (6.0km). On to Bwlch Main, the mountain's sculpture gallery where it displays an assortment of towering crags, gnarled and weathered, standing guard along the summit route.

Then Snowdon peak itself (7.5km, 4.7ml by the ridge route; elevation 1085m, 3560ft).

The circle is complete; each Snowdonia peak in its allotted place, lower; encompassed within a frontier of sea.

Northeastward: the Glyders and Tryfan, guarding Eryri's inner crucible: the lake of secrets, Idwal, keeper of the Ice Age memorybank. Flowing from the crucible: Pen Yr

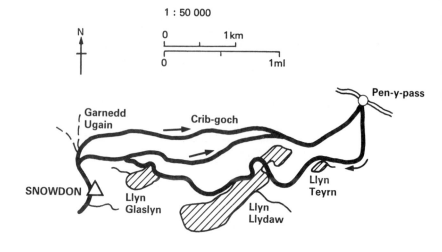

Ole Wen, Dafydd, Llywelyn, heading a long tail of peaks ending in Conwy Mountain, which waits to disclose its dark age legend of the kingdom beneath the sea.

Northwestward: the sea, surrounding the expanse of Ynys Mon, which offers its own Mynydd Twr – Holyhead Mountain – a far satellite on the rim of ocean.

Westward: Mynydd Mawr, astride a mountain door, presiding above a bard's valley.

Southwestward: Moel Hebog, holding within its bulk the story of a rebel hero's retreat.

Southward: the sea, Eryri's export route for dispersal to the world of its very own slate.

Southeastward: the Cnicht, knight of a Saxon vision; the Moelwyns, symbol of the Ffestiniogs.

Eastward: Moel Siabod, standing apart from its fellow peaks; weather beacon; herald of Snowdonia to the eastern land mass.

An inverse of the city street.

The eyes just peer and peer as vision expands, relaying to the mind a perception that seeks an adjustment of perspective. Here, the earth is supreme, in full command of all its heritage, in total self possession, assured of its purpose and its destiny.

gnarled bank

Of course, the premier peak deserves a multi-approach if its flavour is to be savoured.

Strike out from the summit (0.0km) north-northwestward along the ridge, possibly with a bracing wind sweeping up the precipitous western slope, hustling a billowing mist. Escape is available through a gap NE (0.6km), plunging down eastward, clinging to a cliff face that is Crib-y-ddysgl's southern bulwark.

Or, if feeling inspired, ignore the gap and continue northward then NE along the top of this mass of cliff and boulder to the Crib's centre-piece, Garnedd Ugain, only sixty-five feet (20m) short of the premier peak and enjoying the distinction of offering isolation, being very much less visited, though not lacking views of at least equal magnificence. The ridge route bears eastward to Crib-goch, sailing above plunging cliffs and then descending steeply down to join the Pig Track which winds along to the south beneath those self-same cliffs. The young earth might have suffered a crisis here when a convulsing mass of molten metal met fetid air turning it to solid rock. There is a sound of a waterfall, flowing everlastingly from primordial times, suggesting the sea's distant rumination on the eternity of its fate. Williams Parry suggests:

iii.   Chwery drwmp uwch rhaeadr yt
                   A'i nerth sydd lawen wrthyt.

                   Play a trumpet above the falls
                   And its force makes you happy.

If the mist withdraws its veil another world may be revealed far below, a lakeland world disporting on the mountain's plateau.

The Pig Track plunges down from the Crib-goch ridge into Llanberis Pass whose function is to separate this mountain landscape from the one northward, the Glyders and their entourage, which will enter this story in due course. Meanwhile, there is Pen-y-pass and its cosy, well-equipped youth hostel (7.7km, 4.8ml), host to walkers from all corners of the globe at some time or other.

From Pen-y-pass (0.0km) southward along the Miners' track, the mountains may be indulging their habit of synthesis, like primeval volcanoes. The action may take the form of a mist play, the set being a sharply defined ridge silhouetted against a sky that is momentarily lucid; or perhaps revealing a distant cloud mountain, stacked high towards the stratosphere, rivalling these terrestrial mountains. The precipice below the ridge could be bathed in light, brazenly representing itself as an inhabitant of a distant desert. Then a teasing action follows with a raising of shrouds in one place, revealing cliff faces and ridges standing proud, and a simultaneous lowering in another place, obscuring what was clear. The play may be called: Nothing Stays the Same for Long in Eryri, Especially the Weather.

distant weather cock

A rectangular ruin by the shore of Llyn Teyrn (1.8km) sets one trying to imagine the lives of those who once lived there. Rigorous lives, no doubt; certainly isolated in our terms, though mitigated in theirs by a hardy independence and a special sense of community. Community? Where are the remains? Oral history and legend. Bobl Mynydd – the mountain people – lived with an enduring pride in their self-reliance that forged special characteristics, differentiating them from valley people.

One marches on suspecting that something of quality has been lost.

Llyn Llydaw presents its grand sophisticated sweep at the feet of towering creigiau that watch jealously over their prize as one crosses the causeway and strolls along the shore. It is deceptive ease. Onward, upward, westward, northwestward to Llyn Glaslyn – the green lake – a deep, dark green unless the sky be clear and it seeks to become blue in spite of sombre crags overlooking it. And then, above a curvacious

Yr Wyddfa's Glaslyn

northern inlet, is another rectangular ruin, much larger than the one by Llyn Teyrn, a mature establishment facing south with steps leading down to the lake. There the coracles would have been moored, ready for the daily task of providing a fresh haul from the lake. One imagines a spacious kitchen and parlour with animals securely housed during the winter months at the end of the building. Women relinquished their tasks to give birth and the newborn opened their eyes upon this lake and those jagged ridges. This was their world: everything beyond was mystery. Somewhere towards the setting sun was a high mountain peak known as Yr Wyddfa, a place of mystery. To reach it required a steep climb.

Before departing we can discover the origin of the Miners' Track. It is to the east of the ruin. Miners trudged this way to work and could not have imagined why folk would want to do it for pleasure.

Seek as you will for an easy way up via the western shore of Llyn Glaslyn, there is no escaping the steep climb NW, starting just west of the ruin, scrambling over scree, then looping westward and up again to join the route of the Pig Track (6.5km).

The climb across closely packed contours becomes increasingly a trek towards fantasy. Or, so it seems, if mist shrouds the entire landscape isolating the climber in a singular world of sensual impressions. Could there be a train on the ridge? A steam train? In the memory there is a Chekhovian play, Wild Honey, the first written by the great dramatist.

iv. "In the darkness before the scene commences there is the sound of a goods train, clanking and whistling as it passes through the auditorium. The red tail light of the train appears at the front of the stage, moving away from us. The stage lights up to reveal the smoke left by the locomotive, with the tail light disappearing amongst it."

A steam train at the premier peak seems as likely as one in an auditorium. As one comes up through the gap onto the ridge, there it is! Red lights in the mist. Clanking and whistling. And puffing. A whiff of smoke on the ridge.

After exertions of the climb, enjoy a cooling west wind while making for the peak (8.5km, 5.3ml).

Inspiration? Imagine the visual display – peaks, ridges, valleys, cwms, rivers and lakes, all set against the sky and sea – translated into art. The art of painting and music. In painting: what drama might be captured and conveyed through time? In music: what intensity of feeling could be composed for interpretation in nuance of mood?

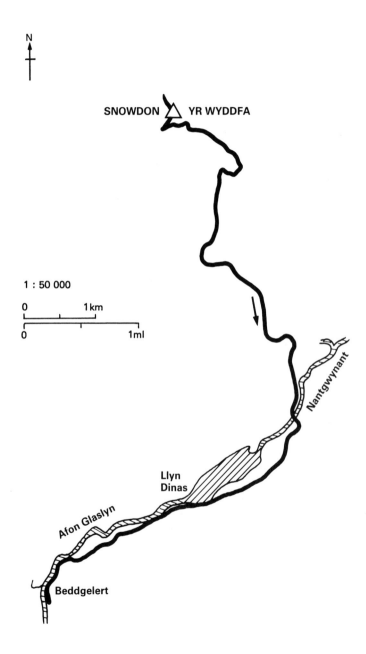

SNOWDON YR WYDDFA

1 : 50 000

Nantgwynant

Llyn
Dinas

Afon Glaslyn

Beddgelert

Southwestward along the ridge from the peak (0.0km) is the point of descent down the Watkin Path – so called after Edward Watkin who originated it, and named by William Gladstone in 1892.

There is something sobering about descent, requiring uncommon steadiness. The peaks are places of fantasy, where sublime thoughts may be released without embarrassment. On a summit ridge one dares to imagine, conceive, resolve. Moses laboured on Mount Sinai to produce what could never have been evolved on a plain. The imagination surges, then must be brought down to face . . . what might well be a withering experience.

Retaining inspiration is not so difficult, one discovers, when descending to Nantgwynant, a village successfully nurturing an air of seclusion despite being a junction of pathways, ancient and modern. For thousands of years paths have extended from Nantgwynant westward, northward, eastward, southward. These routes are still here, and because of the topography of the locality it may be reasonably safe to assume that their future will extend at least as far as their past. How re-assuring to feel such confidence!

Southward from the PO, turn left from the road over the bridge, then right, past the farmhouse, Llyndy-isaf (9.3km). Here is a chance to enjoy a quiet valley path beside lakes and a river that owe their existence to Snowdon, for they begin life up there near the peak. A stream flows from the summit massif into Llyn Glaslyn and acquires its name from the lake. It tumbles into the majestic Llyn Llydaw where it basks idly for a while, sometimes playing with reflections when the wind departs. Leaving its host quietly, it picks up volume and speed, spills over the crags of Cwm Dyli, meanders to the valley floor, forms itself into a broad channel in service of Llyn Gwynant where it enjoys the devotions of an endless troupe of beauty gazers. Not content with these conquests it seeks further admiration in Llyn Dinas; all of which is preliminary to the triumphs awaiting it lower down in the Aberglaslyn Pass.

For the time being we leave the Glaslyn at Beddgelert (14.5km, 9.1ml), cross the bridge and from the PO (0.0km)

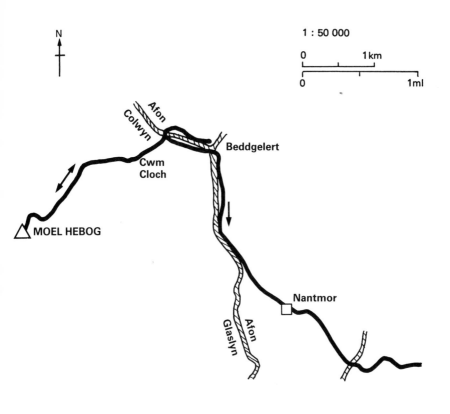

continue W along the A4085 to a left turn over the Afon Colwyn which began its life on the opposite side of Snowdon from the birthplace of the Afon Glaslyn. Southwestward to Cwm Cloch farmhouse then westward and southwestward.

Seeking the bald peak of Moel Hebog (4.8km, 3ml; elevation 782m, 2566ft) is to tread sacred ground of Owain Glyndwr. Not a seat commemorating the hours of triumph. For that one must travel to Machynlleth where the insurrectionary Prince of all Wales summoned a Parliament in 1403–4, and, in the manner of a ruling monarch with supreme power at his disposal, concluded a treaty with the King of France.

We tread the territory of defeat when rebellion had failed, the cause lost and Owain was a fugitive in hiding, his accommodation the lonely cave of his name, Ogof Owain Glyndwr, which lies beneath this summit. Supplies were organised, so it was said, by the Prior of Beddgelert, though nothing could save the rebel leader who was much too proud to accept a pardon which the English king proferred. Perhaps his defiance to the end is the reason for the unique place he holds in Welsh tradition and imagination.

Looking back in time from this desolate decline beneath Moel Hebog to the turn of the fifteenth century we find Owain Glyndwr as a wealthy landowner of Glyndyfrdwy, receiving a rent roll of two hundred pounds a year, a considerable income which made him one of the richest Welshmen of his day, and of at least equal in standing to the English marcher lords who were his immediate enemies.

The great rebellion of 1400 began as a local squabble over a piece of land, an incident which may be compared to women rioting in a Petrograd bread queue sparking the Russian revolution in February 1917, or colonists throwing tea into Boston harbour in 1773, starting the American War of Independence. Glyndwr received a summons to serve in a war which the king was waging against the Scots. In refusing to respond to the summons he provoked reaction from the Lord Marcher in North Wales, Lord Grey of Ruthin, who tried to arrest him. Glyndwr eluded Grey and launched a counter-attack. Support for Glyndwr flowed throughout Wales, as did the tide of battle.

How might have events turned from those victorious times when the rebels held power over most of Wales? With hindsight – extending to six hundred years! – two ifs may be proposed. If Glyndwr had avoided fractious attacks upon his people and, instead, had nurtured their unity; if he had sought a sensible compromise while holding the initiative in battle, could the rebellion have succeeded?

On another peak, not dissimilar in configuration to Moel Hebog, we shall take opportunity to compare Owain's experience with that of another Welsh leader, and, from the wider world, focus on two figures who led similar kinds of struggle.

Cnicht

9.7km 7.1ml

From Beddgelert PO (0.0km), E along the A4085, turn right over the bridge and immediately left to the footbridge spanning the Afon Glaslyn, and right, along the river bank to a footbridge 700m downstream. Here we meet a remnant of one of the most incredible creations in Snowdonia: the track of the Welsh Highland Railway.

It seems like a fairy tale. A steam train running from Porthmadog through the Aberglaslyn Pass to Beddgelert, on to Rhyd-ddu, past Llyn Cwellyn, looping westward near Waunfawr into picturesque countryside south of Glan-yr-afon where the line forked, one track veering southward to slate quarries near Bryngwyn, the other continuing westward to a junction at Dinas where travellers, sated with scenic enjoyment, could complete their journey to Caernarfon.

Now imagine a stroke of magic in which this entire line was restored, including its incredible steam locomotives bearing such names as Karen, Pedemoura, Nantmor, Russell, Moel Tryfan. Would such an attraction not draw passengers in hundreds of thousands from locations worldwide? This was not the dominant vision which motivated a small group of enthusiasts who came together in 1961. They wanted to engage in a restoration which they felt to be immensely worthwhile in itself.

The original Welsh Highland Railway had been opened in 1923 and closed in 1937 because of competition from road transport. Its rebirth would entail a long, hard slog from the formation of the new Welsh Highland Light Railway Company (1964) Ltd to the opening of part of the line, from Porthmadog to Pen y Mount, in August 1980. Walking along the bed of the track through the Aberglaslyn Pass into two short tunnels then a 300m tunnel, we may imagine a railway passenger's delight. Almost certainly, too, we shall lament destruction of a wonderful facility, and feel encouraged that an operation exists dedicated to its restoration.

Beyond the tunnel is a stile (2.4km) and a road (2.6km) where we turn left to Nantmor (2.8km).

This village is a reminder that change is perpetual, including that which results from physical interaction on the earth's surface. The name suggests the evolution. Nantmor, or Nanmor, derives from Nant-y-mor, gorge or brook by the sea. In earlier times the sea washed up here, covering Traeth Mawr – Big Beach – to the north of Porthmadog, submerging much of what is now Penrhyndeudraeth. Norman English castles – Conwy, Beaumaris, Caernarfon, Harlech – were built on what was then the coastline so as to be supplied by sea which the conquerors commanded. Will the sea return one day? Probably. And to a higher level if the increasing presence of carbon-dioxide in the atmosphere and impairment of the ozone layer continue to raise earth temperatures thereby melting polar ice. So, Nantmor could again become Nant-y-mor.

The Roman road lay this way by the sea, though there is no feel of the ancient route until well beyond Nantmor. Leaving Bwlchgwernog (4.4km) the path bears S up a hill, then E/NE, SE and eastward. In the rugged beauty of this wild terrain Roman auxiliary infantry may be imagined tramping along in bronze helmets, iron-mail shirts as body armour, with scarves at the neck to prevent chafing. Hobnailed sandals would be the only disturbance to an immense peace and quiet.

The track leads SE to Croesor (6.7km) but to reach the Cnicht we bear left (6.1km) and continue northeastward to a stile (6.5km) and 200m further on, bear E veering to 070°, to 130° (6.9km) and a stile (7.0km). Turn left (060°) onto the ridge.

Who can doubt the reason for its popularity? Up ahead is an isosceles triangle representing itself as a classical peak offering genuine challenge. The approach guarantees respect: the ridge rising towards the sky like the upward pitching deck of an aircraft carrier. On the right is the great chasm of Cwm Croesor and beyond it the bald pate of Moel-

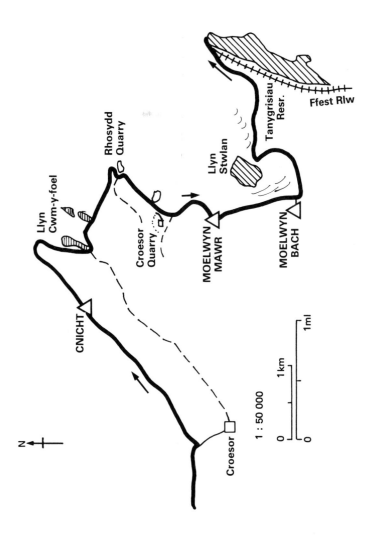

wyn Mawr. Reaching the base of the isosceles triangle massif (9.0km) and commencing its ascent, one feels suspicion of hidden intent, remembering that mountains have a habit of appearing forthright, displaying a clear impression while proffering false summits which the climber joyfully greets only to discover the real one brazenly proclaiming itself further on. But no, there the peak is (9.7km, 6.1ml; elevation 690m, 2265ft), standing bold, sharp and true to its name, The Cnicht, which derives from the old spelling used by the Saxons who must have been impressed by the sight of this knight appearing on the horizon.

The way ahead from the knight's pinnacle is northeastward veering to 080° along the ridge. Veer round eastward, steeply down into the cwm, southward and southwestward to a stream flowing down the Cnicht's steep redoubt.

Llyn Cwm-y-foel – lake of the bald top cwm – when viewed on a sunny day from afar, say from the top of the ridge dividing the Nantgwynant and Ffestiniog Valleys, can be imagined, romantically, as symbolising Snowdonia: nestling in the mountains with a distant view of the sea on the horizon. At its weir (12.7km), temptation descends from opposite directions. To the southwest is a footbridge (15.0km), a farm track to a village road (16.3km) leading to Croesor (17.3km) which, despite all the pressures of this century, retains the atmosphere of a distant mountain village. When contemporary ravages are exhausted, Croesor will tell a story of continuity through countless ages, a story of assimilation and enduring character.

In the opposite direction – to the northeast and east – lies a different story.

The Moelwyns

4.7km   2.9ml.   7.0km   4.4ml.

From Llyn Cwm-y-foel weir (0.0km) eastward beyond
the ridge lies Llynnau Dyffryn – valley lakes. Skirting the
southernmost shore (0.7km) there is an easy passage along
the contour eastward to a quarry track which bears southeastward onto the deck of the old Rhosydd Quarries and
towards the ruin of the quarry buildings (2.6km). The men
who worked these and neighbouring quarries radiated from
the shore of tranquil Llyn Cwmorthin. There the ruined
chapel marks what was the community's centre of focus.

South of Rhosydd Quarry building a quarrymen's path
leads SW towards Croesor Quarry, which, in its heyday, was
orientated not towards the Cwmorthin chapel – though little
more than half a mile separated the two quarries – but to its
home base, Croesor village. After several decades of decline, economic depression in the early nineteen-thirties
finally halted operations in these upland quarries, leaving to
nature the more protracted task of assimilating the remains
of industrial activity. That stage not having yet been
reached, we may use the Croesor Quarry building as a land-
mark, bearing SW from it, then S and southeastward, and
finally southwestward again.

The bald Moelwyn Mawr peak (4.7km, 2.9ml; elevation
770m, 2527ft) offers no intrinsic mystery. Indeed, its trian-
gulation station sprouts incongruously from the featureless
top. Interest is external, in the views it commands of lakes,
ridges, peaks and the sea. And, within that range, the
opportunity it offers to continue an appraisal of historical
characters.

On a bearing of 280° we may sight Moel Hebog holding
the secret of Ogof Owain Glyndwr and the hero's retreat in
defeat. In almost the opposite direction, bearing 140°, there
is Tomen-y-mur, southeast of Ffestiniog, where Gruffydd ap
Cynan, Prince of Gwynedd, turned the tide against the Nor-

man English King, William Rufus. Gruffydd and Owain were 300 years apart in time besides being contrasting in character, attitude and achievement. From the wider world, the records of two other historical characters are available for comparison.

George Washington's emergence as commander of American rebel forces near Boston in 1775, and the town's capture after a vigorous siege, was a notable summit on a long timescale of unspectacular operations. For Washington, education and training had been an on-the-job apprenticeship in colonial wars against the French and Indians (1754–63). This was an inglorious period involving as much losing as winning, and nothing in the way of generally remembered achievement. Presumably, though, the future first President of the United States must have gained useful experience which he was able to apply much later when he was at the head of an army. That included years when rebel forces were in retreat, and despair threatened disintegration. Goethe, Germany's greatest poet, also a scientist and statesman, and a contemporary of Washington, penned a proverb which begs recollection. "Character is best formed in the stormy billows of the world; talents are best nurtured in solitude." After more than five years of reverses and defeats, also involving acute deprivation and starvation, the victory at Yorktown and the surrender of the imperial army, must have seemed like a most incredible deliverance.

On the other side of the world, Mikhail Kutuzov was less fortunate than George Washington in having to serve not a rebel army that knew what it stood for and loved what it knew – to paraphrase Cromwell – but the Czar of All Russia who kept pressurising him into fighting battles which Kutuzov knew could not be won and, therefore, should not be fought. Like Washington he gained an initial training in the arts of war as a soldier in the ranks, fighting inglorious colonial wars against Poles and Turks (1764–74) which do not now feature on history's illuminated memorybank. As a result of losing battles he did not want to fight, Kutuzov was dismissed from his post in disgrace and retired to his country estate. Washington also spent a middle period on his Virginia estate though that was entirely voluntary in consequence of there being no more urgent call upon his services. Invasion of Russia by Napoleon in 1812 created a very urgent demand for Kutuzov to take command of Russian forces. Even so, he was still subject to interference from Czar Alexander who obliged him to fight the battle of Boridino, which was lost, opening the way for the French to take Moscow. So serious had the situation become that Kutuzov was, at last, given a free hand. He blocked Napoleon's chosen retreat route, forcing him to withdraw over devastated territory in mid-winter – all without committing large forces to a major battle.

Gruffydd ap Cynan had been through a similar experience 700 years earlier. Gruffydd had spent twenty years fighting to secure the kingdom of Gwynedd, suffering defeat and imprisonment, but slowly and patiently putting together the political conditions that enabled him to secure Gwynedd in 1094 with support from the whole of Wales. He was now ready to face the Norman English whose leader, William Rufus, nurtured the intention of conquering Wales before the winter of 1095. As with Kutuzov, Gruffydd avoided direct confrontation. He commanded an orderly retreat as Rufus advanced from Chester, harrying him, cutting supply lines, engaging the kind of strategy and tactics which later became known as guerrilla warfare. Gruffydd established a fallback position at Tomen-y-mur where the momentum of his enemy's thrust reached its limit. Rufus was obliged to retreat – all the way to Chester – with Gruffydd in pursuit.

Under Gruffydd there followed a period of peace, material fruitfulness and cultural renaissance exemplified in an output of poetry from bards who came to be known as The Poets of the Princes. It lasted forty years. Wales remained unconquered for almost 200 years.

Leaving Moelwyn Mawr peak (4.7km) bear southeastward down a steep slope into Craigysgafn, a rocky ridge with a precipitous drop offering a considerable surprise. If accustomed to thinking of Llyn Stwlan as a high-altitude storage reservoir, what is one to make of seeing it far below one's feet? Memorable exhilaration: a descent of nature's sculp-

45

ture above the world's broad beam! Down, down, then up, up. Southeastward, then southwestward and westward, up to Moelwyn Bach peak (7.0km, 4.4ml; elevation 711m, 2334ft). It has a structure that makes one suspect that it may also have a soul. Back from the peak, eastward, there is a gallery of symbolistic sculpture. One moves down a slope with rock artwork on either side just as in a fabricated gallery, observing the exhibits, wondering what to make of them, what message they convey into the perplexities of our times. With these sculptures the gallery will remain perpetually open and the exhibits available for interpretation through aeons of time.

The descent eastward then southward leads to a more accustomed view of Llyn Stwlan. Treading traditional paths that were here long before the dam, the hydro-electric scheme or the snake-like road with its countless hairpin bends, one arrives below Stwlan lake (8.8km) that once owed its life solely to the natural waters flowing off the Moelwyns. That was before 1957 when the Central Electricity Generating Board commenced work on what was to become one of the largest pumped storage schemes in the world. We may now judge the result of that endeavour.

Turn right (120°) and continue to a stile (9.1km) that marks an old path down to Tanygrisiau. This route chooses the quarry tramway (070°), offering steep slopes and a passage between two pairs of giant piers towards the cuboid shape of the power station sitting by the shore of the lake. No chemicals rising into the air; no fouling discharges into the lake where trout are said to thrive; no noise. Ffestiniog's propensity for producing vast quantities of rain water seems to have been put to a worthwhile use, creating, incidentally, a limitless potential for educational observation, besides restoring Tanygrisiau to the economic map from which it had slipped when quarrying was eclipsed in the nineteen-thirties. All based upon the process of drawing off-peak power from the grid to pump water from the lower to the higher lake from which the turbines will be powered during the following peak supply period.

Another power phenomenon seeks our attention! When its steam whistle blows the whole valley knows it is on the move, making another incredible journey. The red lights on the crossing begin flashing. More whistling as it departs from Tanygrisiau station: it is over the crossing and on its way, pacing the length of the lake. Instinctively, one raises both hands in a joyous wave; driver and passengers wave back. The waving continues until the train is out of sight. And then there is a feeling that in those spontaneous exchanges of warm greetings between total strangers lay a significant message.

Why does one feel so exhilarated? Yes, the Ffestiniog Railway is a triumph of imagination, idealism, courage, persistence, determination, innovation. Should one add modesty? At any rate, a triumph of all those human characteristics is certainly worthy of celebration.

What happened between 1946 when the Ffestiniog Railway was closed, and 1955 when a section of line was reopened by volunteers using an original 1863 steam locomotive? Why were those volunteers not heedful of warnings that the enterprise would not be financially viable, profits could not be made; that there were enormous technical difficulties which were virtually insuperable? In a period when the age of mass tourism was not yet visible, what courage was required to withstand accepted realities of the real world? The volunteers would, perhaps, disclaim courage. They believed in an ideal: that the Ffestiniog steam railway was worth all the sacrifices involved in restoration, worth working together for years and years until the objective was achieved. Who would now deny that they were right?

From a footbridge (10.7km), veer left (060°) to a stile and footbridge (11.0km), continue to the CEGB Centre (11.8km), on to the railway station (12.0km) and into the village.

"Under the stairs" was a packhorsemen's description of this location which attached itself as Tanygrisiau in Welsh long before the age of quarrying.

Packhorsemen's ponies had to "climb the stairs" to reach the trails over the mountains leading down to the Nantgwynant Valley. Later, quarrymen's houses appeared also to be climbing the stairs, clinging to the steep slopes. However, the unique atmosphere one feels here in Tanygrisiau seems to have more to do with the steam railway. Spanning the entire length of the village at a high level, it is present everywhere as we continue northeastward past the post office (12.5km).

Turn right (13.0km) from the road to a bridge over a stream which, lower down, becomes the Afon Goedol. Beyond a stile is another at the side of the B4414; turn left and 300m along the road, veer right onto a path, right and then left past the square to a hump-backed bridge where Blaenau Ffestiniog's railway story is displayed. Beyond the bridge turn right to the centre of town (14.7km, 9.2ml).

Blaenau Ffestiniog's difference compared with any other town could not have been planned. It is simply the way it has happened. Loss of an industry that sustained a community for more than a century might have resulted in decimation. Not so here. Here, character, allied with atmosphere, is everything.

The forbears of rhododendron plants growing wild around Blaenau were transported from half a world away and proliferate in a favourable climate. Similarly, seekers after inspiration arrive and sense opportunities.

The arts flourish; arts in every form nurtured from a spiritual wellspring, the source of which can be as elusive as that of a mountain spring.

The traditional Welsh art forms are most pre-eminent. Compression of dispersed rural communities into an industrial town concentrated the musical art so durably that it has thrived by adaptation to the big fundamental change in the economic life of the town. The Royal Oakley Silver Band, once "the poor man's introduction to music" with a membership consisting entirely of quarrymen, now enrols mainly teenagers who wish to use musical talents which tuition in school has developed. Membership in either of Blaenau's two choirs – Cor Meibion y Moelwyn and Y Brythoniaid – requires performance to international standard; a capacity to render in several languages; a preparedness to accept engagements anywhere in Britain or abroad. Blaenau is accustomed to seeing its musical artists winning top prizes and being accepted as first-rank performers. In setting out to scale the higher levels of Blaenau the ideal would be to take a sample of such performance: to imbibe as part of the total experience.

A choice of route to the next peak, Moel Siabod, via this prospectus, takes in Dolwyddelan, one of Eryri's significant pathway junctions. Two main routes are available, each with variations within themselves. The western route lies through the upper Lledr Valley, possessed of romantic scenery that contrasts markedly with other parts of this peaks route, and includes Dolwyddelan Castle as an option. The eastern route crosses the quarry scene and lakeland above Blaenau, and plunges down into Cwm Penamnen at the bottom of which is Dolwyddelan.

The Western Route

From the Blaenau PO (0.0km) walk E/SE along the A470 for almost 200m, take the third turning left and continue N, following the quarry road as it curves eastward between hills of slate debris. Turn left (1.0km) across the route of an old tramway and follow the road NW. Before reaching a quarry building, about 500m further on, turn right and maintain a north bearing beyond the quarry workings to a gate and stile at the base of Ffridd-y-bwlch (2.4km). Continue uphill on a bearing of 350°, skirting the corner of a fence, to the left summit (2.7km). From the vantage point of this half-size peak (473m, 1550ft), consider the visual image which Blaenau presents to the world.

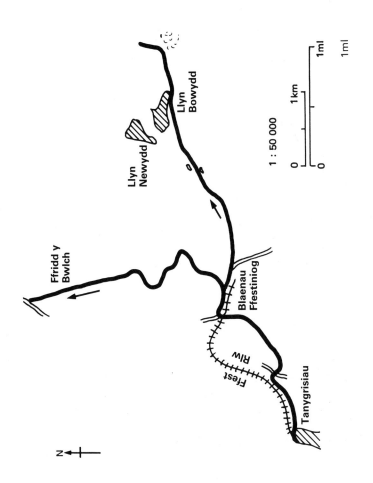

Ffridd y Bwlch

Llyn Newydd

Llyn Bowydd

Blaenau Ffestiniog

Ffest Riw

Tanygrisiau

N

1 : 50 000

0   1km

0   1ml

1ml

Mountains are turned inside out, quarry levels are exposed, the workplace scene remains much as it was when the last shift knocked off. If the eye of the beholder is predisposed to look upon the consequences of industrialism with disfavour, such predisposition may be challenged here where there is a message of vitality. Dereliction and depression may apply elsewhere. Here the action is suspended, poised, awaiting the next signal, aware that a continuing operation does exist. Meanwhile, almost two centuries of labour is distilled into art for conveyance through time.

Continue down to the A470 (3.6km), cross the road, follow the track northward passing Moel Dyrnogydd on the left, out onto an elevated platform that feels suspended on an S-bend (5.3km) above the upper Lledr. Below, on the right, the Afon Gorddinan gushes; on the left is the massive hump of Moel Siabod, while in the centre, on a bearing of 060°, is the keep of Dolwyddelan Castle.

The track SW from the S-bend leads towards a miniature tower which is an air shaft of the railway tunnel far beneath (6.3km). This is part of the magic which a train traveller on the Blaenau to Llandudno line experiences. Leaving Blaenau the train plunges into a long tunnel at the end of which is a different world – the upper Lledr.

Continue northeastward and northward to the tunnel mouth (8.2km), on through a railway culvert (8.6km) to a farmhouse, Hendre (9.2km), to a turn right 300m further on. Continue eastward to a fence stile (10.0km), on past a cottage (Aber) and over a footbridge to a bridge that spans the railway. Turn left over the bridge and continue along wheeltracks to the farmhouse, Gorddinan (11.0km). At the end of the farm drive there is a choice of route.

For the castle route fork left over the railway, and over Pont Sarn-ddu – black causeway – otherwise known as Roman Bridge – or Pont Rhufain – which spans the Afon Lledr. A fine old bridge with rectangular piers carrying massive stone lintels and long timbers across eight spans. From it, northeastward, we reach farm outbuildings at Penrhiw (11.9km) where a turn right (080°) onto a track offers a most attractive approach, at eye-level, to the castle. If one can

black causeway

53

exclude distractions southward and eastward, a sense of the thirteenth century may be experienced.

Dolwyddelan Castle, together with Dolbadarn near Llanberis, and Cricieth Castle, represent the power of the Welsh princes in the twelfth and thirteenth centuries prior to the conquest of 1282–3 when other, more formidable, castles were added to the landscape around Eryri. Approaching this Welsh castle, a residence of Llywelyn Fawr and a headquarters of Llywelyn ap Gruffydd during the conquest period, thoughts of heritage are apt to rise again.

The late medieval period of castles, knights and shining armour, inhabit a romantic world that is now synonymous with fantasy. No anger or resentment stirs in the breast when looking upon an example of that remote period: we can contemplate it with an entirely benign eye. Whether this could eventually lead to a movement for castle restoration may be a moot point.

From the north side of the castle the track leads E/SE down to the A470 (13.7km), turn left and continue to Dolwyddelan PO (14.5km), the starting point for the ascent of Siabod.

An alternative to the castle route and road walk is available at the fork on the south side of the Roman Bridge at the end of the Gorddinan farm drive. Take the right fork and continue (SE) across the A470, turn left (NE), past the farmhouse Bertheos and eastward through a delightful part of the valley to Pentre-bont, a hamlet on the south side of the river opposite Dolwyddelan.

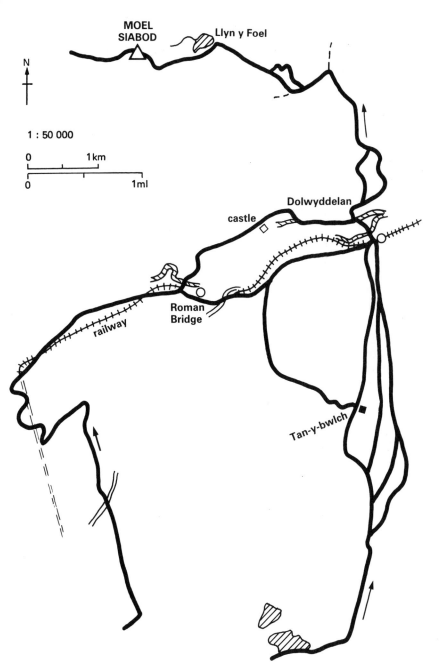

The Eastern Route

From the Blaenau PO (0.0km), walk southeastward, turn left (0.4km) and continue (050°) beyond the end of the street onto a path which winds eastward, veering left to a general bearing of 045° between derelict winding piers (1.9km) and two ponds. Beyond a wall ladder (2.4km) and a fence stile (2.6km) the track joins an old quarry tramway (3.0km) by the southern shore of Llyn Bowydd reservoir.

Turn eastward along the quarry tramway track to the ruin of a barrack-like building (4.1km), once the weekday (Mondays to Saturdays) living quarters of quarrymen working the faces round about. Northward 200m is one such pit. We pass it and continue to the boundary of the Forestry Commission plantation (5.3km). This is a quarrymen's path, the travel-to-work route used for about a century up to the nineteen-thirties. Then the hillsides would have been bare or carrying a sparse selection of hardwoods. Now, almost the entire surface of Cwm Penamnen, into which we are descending, is clothed in a uniform deep green of Sitka Spruce, invariable throughout the year.

We descend, and may enjoy a choice of route by courtesy of the forestry roads which flake out along the length of Cwm Penamnen. Roman use of this route is assumed in the name Sarn Helen. If we wish to follow in their tracks we should choose the western side of the cwm passing the house Ty'n-y-cwm. Who was Helen? A Roman commander's wife? Or, a local Boadicea who led a rebellion against the Romans? There is a Ffynnon Helen – Helen's Spring – near Croesor where her army is said to have rested, and Rhyd yr Helen – Helen's Ford – which is further to the south on this Roman route connecting the forts at Tomen-y-mur, southeast of Ffestiniog, and Caer Llugwy, west of Betws-y-coed.

If the Sitka Spruce becomes too oppressive, there is a relief option at Tan-y-bwlch, an old cottage almost opposite the farmhouse, Gwyndy. Turn left (300°) up the wall of the cwm into a dark tunnel through the plantation. Time for contemplation, recalling that this old track zigzagged up a hillside spread with wild flowers. Perhaps the pleasure felt by walkers then would compare with relief felt now when one emerges from the tunnel, over the boundary stile at the top to a brilliant view of Yr Wyddfa and her attendant Crib Goch, and the Lledr Valley captivatingly displayed in the foreground.

The descent is exhilarating, tempting one to run down hill past a corlan-cerrig – a walled enclosure for livestock – on past a ruined cottage on the left, forking right to join the path from Roman Bridge, and on to Pentre-bont and a confluence of routes down Cwm Penamnen to Dolwyddelan (10.7km). Opportunities extend in all directions from this large meadow – Gwyddelan's meadow – near the heart of Eryri, a natural magnet, junction, meeting place. In these respects little has changed since St Gwyddelan arrived in the sixth century. The fertile meadow, host to a sparkling river rich in trout and salmon, sheltered within a mountain stronghold: all this is immutable through centuries of time. Only a railway and a main road have been added. And houses that were once occupied by quarrymen and their families. If a new purpose is being sought, one is already available. A centre for exploring an incomparable network the delights of which await realisation.

v.　　　　　A thrum aruthr. Â'm morwyn
　　　Esgyn wnaf innau'n ysgawn i fynydd,
　　　Yntau yn wridog tan yr ehedydd;
　　　　Ymwelwa grug y moelydd pan ger bron
　　　Yr aeddfed aeron rodd haf i'w deurudd.

　　　　　Enticing peak. With my girl
　　　I ascend eagerly to the mountain,
　　　Its rugged face glowing beneath the larks;
　　　　The summit heather pales alongside
　　　The beauty of summer upon her cheeks.

Moel Siabod

7.5km   4.7ml

From the PO (0.0km) bear NW up the lane, turn right (E) through a critch-cratch, left (0.2km) across a field (040°) to a stile (0.4km). Here we may choose between a fishermen's path and a packhorse trail.

The fishermen's path

From the stile (0.4km) turn left and continue northward over stiles (0.7km and 0.8km) and on to the plantation boundary (1.0km). Into the plantation 150m there is a footbridge over the Afon Ystumiau – the winding river – which is Siabod's gift to the valleys. Beyond it is a forest road bridge carrying the route of the old packhorse trail.

The packhorse trail

From the stile at 0.4km continue on 070° to wheeltracks that merge with a forest road (0.9km) which bears northward. Fork left (1.4km) and join the fishermen's path 100m further on, a few metres beyond the forest road bridge over the Afon Ystumiau. Continuing along the forest road, cross the Afon Ystumiau again (2.9km) and, 200m further on, fork left, leaving the packhorse trail which would lead one along the base of Siabod to Capel Curig and the Llugwy Valley.

We are now back on the fishermen's path which, for the time being, is a forest road bearing southwestward. A choice of route is again available – 400m from the fork (3.5km). Taking the right fork, continue to the forest road's end and turn left across the stream, which is again the Afon Ystumiau. This winding river wanders all over the moor and through the plantation before finding its outlet to the Lledr near Dolwyddelan Castle.

By taking the left fork (3.5km) one discovers something about life at the foot of the mountain. Down the track 200m (3.7km), veer right (310°) onto a green path lying between blocks of plantation. There is a confluence of streams (4.1km) – the Afon Ystumiau again – and above it the ruin of a cottage which would once have been located in open moorland. The family might have lived off fish, chickens, ducks, geese, sheep, pigs, a cow or two. Once a week some members of the family – probably the wife and one or two of her children – would have walked down to Dolwyddelan or Capel Curig to offer produce for sale and make purchases. A journey as far as Betws-y-coed would have been an unusual event. The husband and sons may have found work in the quarry up on the mountain. Lying beneath the plantation there is an old path bearing northward from near the house towards the quarry. One of the reasons for the quarry continuing in operation until 1940, when most others in the area had been closed a decade earlier, was its high-quality product, the sulphur content of the slate being exceptionally low. The men may have lived during the week in the company barracks on the mountain, leaving the women to work the holding. Possibly they sustained two jobs: rising in the dark hours of morning to attend to the animals; a walk to the quarry for start of work at seven; a walk back after finishing at five-thirty; a couple of hours work on the holding; then supper and bed.

Take the cottager's path from the west side of the ruin to join the path, 200m up the hill, across the stream from the end of the forest road. Turn left (W) and continue to a stile at the plantation boundary. In shedding the overburden of the plantation we enter the realm of virgin streams crashing over waterfalls, or secluded places between heather-covered rocks. A hideaway for the bard and his love?

vi.   Dyriau gludai'r awel
            A sawr y maes ar ei mel.
            Ac nid oedd gerllaw un bronfraith tawel,
            Na diwedd i hoen ehedydd anwel.

            The breeze carried quiet song
            Through the taste of her magic.
            Not soft melody of a singing thrush,
            A vivacious trill of a hidden lark.

This is nature's original design right to the source of the Afon Ystumiau at Llyn y Foel – the lake of the bald top. Of modest size, hidden in rugged peacefulness beyond reach of the world except for hardy footsloggers resolved upon venturing this way, Siabod's own lake cradled in its crooked arm, is a fishermen's perfect retreat. One's eye ranges up toward the peak and down again to the lake, conscious of a distinction that settled upon this mountain.

One day in early March 1934 "when the snow was still on the Foel" a quarryman, who had spent his working life in the Siabod Quarry, wandered up here to Llyn y Foel and decided to continue up towards the peak. As was his habit when walking, he kept a keen eye on the flora, a trait inherited from his grandfather who had assembled a collection of rare ferns growing on the higher levels of Eryri. On this afternoon, Evan Roberts spotted pretty purple blooms growing amongst a cluster of rocks. Although unaware of it at the time, he had discovered Tormaen Cyferbynddail – Saxifraga oppositifolia – Purple Saxafrage. It was a discovery that changed his life and was to have a significant effect upon awareness of rare alpine flora of Snowdonia.

A process of discovery and self-discovery had begun, probably beginning with a little-known fact that Eryri was a last retreat of the Ice Age, a place where plants which had adapted to alpine conditions could find refuge. Only in small numbers, of course, because of very real hazards unconnected with their alpine requirements. The process of research into these phenomena was still in its infancy, as only in the last century had an Ice Age presence been recognised. The idea was both incredible and exciting: that there were rare plants which, in some cases, existed only in Eryri, having survived over millennia, bringing their messages and mysteries for decodification.

Evan Roberts was befriended and consulted by persons professionally involved in this field of research; and in due course, he himself joined them. But that was after fortuitous circumstances provided him with opportunities he needed, about which we shall discover more further along this peaks route.

Ascending southwestward, veering round to about 300°, one approaches the peak along the edge of an escarpment which Llyn y Foel drains. The world suddenly opens out revealing itself as a complete circumference of peaks, ridges, sky. At Siabod's peak (7.5km, 4.7ml; elevation 872, 2861ft) the view southwestward towards the sea claims attention, mainly because of the mountain's shape.

Siabod occupies a huge area extending from the Llugwy to the Lledr Valleys and westward to the Pass of Llanberis. Its bulk has a southwesterly tilt providing a long ridge rising from Capel Curig, ending in this elevated vantage point, seaward looking, keeping vigil over the vagaries of weather that is dominated by moods of the western ocean. In its location and aspect, Siabod is Eryri's self-appointed meteorological station, a role that has been accepted down the centuries by those for whom weather is an important daily consideration which may be applied to everybody seeking a living in Eryri. Siabod's signals are perfectly clear and simple. When its peak is shrouded, umbrellas, rainproofs and woollies are the order of the day. A clear Siabod peak gives an assurance that anxieties may be laid to rest – at least until the following morning.

From Siabod peak (0.0km) the rhomboidal lake at Pen-y-gwryd, the objective of this descent, bears 285°. Descending round the boulders one finds, about 100m from the peak, a fence, and along its north side, a stile (0.8km). There is another, 100m further down, which may be disregarded as an optional extra in favour of a fence stile at 2.1km. And now the mind may consider itself liberated for the time being by an omni-presence that demands attention.

Assume a descent into a fresh westerly breeze flowing over the premier peak and its entourage tinged by a declining sun. One is in possession of this vast estate which has been here through aeons of time, more or less in its present state. Such evidence of habitations as may be discernible are mere particles on a distant horizon and may be discounted as a temporary intrusion which nature will assimilate, as indeed it has assimilated Roman roads constructed as recently as the beginning of the first millennium Anno Domini, and is in the process of subjecting the remains of quarrying to similar treatment. A dominant impression is that this estate is of such configuration that humans are not able to damage its essential features. Self-defence appears securely inbuilt; and yet a reservoir of doubt obtrudes. Will another human being – a millennium hence – descend this ridge in full view of a setting sun spreading its colour along the distant coast, lighting the peaks in sharp silhouette against an Arctic sky?

A quarry pit to the north, lower down in Dyffryn Mymbyr, is now barely visible, all but having disappeared into the landscape. Further down, there are remains of what may once have been a boundary wall, now a linear arrangement of ancient stones. After crossing a stile (4.8km) and bearing generally 310° to 5.5km, the line of small boulders again appears. Beyond the stream Nant-y-llys (5.6km) one might never suspect the presence of a key communications centre of the ancient world. Only an anonymous mound remains although, in its heyday, this was an establishment measuring 240 yards by 200 yards enclosing an area of nine-and-a-half acres. As the imperial army's mode of operation allowed troops a day's march between fortified positions, the function of this staging post was to serve the route between Caer

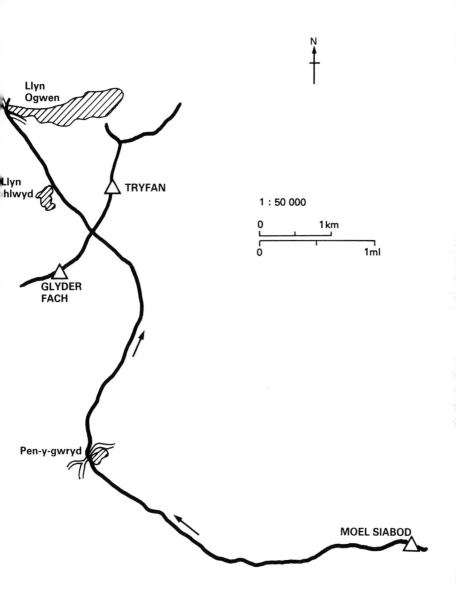

N

Llyn
Ogwen

Llyn
hlwyd

△ TRYFAN

1 : 50 000

0   1 km

0   1 ml

△
GLYDER
FACH

Pen-y-gwryd

MOEL SIABOD △

Llugwy, also known as Bryn Gefeilia, and Segontium. It enabled all the passes to be held and served.

Reaching the stile opposite the Pen-y-gwryd Hotel (7.2km) one is facing the Roman camp's northern boundary.

An interlude. For aesthetic acclimatisation to an experience . . . up near the sky.

Depart from Pen-y-gwryd (0.0km) via a stile opposite the rhomboidal lake, bearing NW across the Afon Nant-y-gwryd which flows down from Llyn Cwm-y-ffynnon – lake of the spring cwm. Bear N and veer to 030° up the rocky side of the massif that supports the Glyders.

The moment of sublimation descends at the point where the rocky bank meets the edge of a grassy plateau (2.7km; elevation 762m, 2500ft) which disports itself as a detached being having a life of its own. Here, one can dally in suspension between different worlds, decline involvement, seek one's soul, form attachments beyond terrestrial planes. The eyes are cast outward and upward in the manner of the bard in a sublime mood.

viii.   Ac edrych uwch llewych lli
         Rhwng haul a'r eang heli
         Ar chwa'r hwyr chwery o aidd
         Ym mhluf y cwmwl hafaidd.
     Rhagom ail-esyd rhyw gymyl isel
     Ar ansawdd caerau. Ynysoedd cwrel
         Ar hyn a chwyth o'r anwel. Ac yn awr
     Mal hud eurog wawr ymleda'r gorwel.

         Looking up at flowing light
         Between sun and vast ocean
         Gentle breezes laugh and play
         In feathers of summery cloud.
     Subtending cloud rebuilds itself
     In the manner of forts. Coral islands
         Then blow from the invisible. And now
     Like dawn's golden magic vision expands.

A communion with sky here, inducing special poignancy, sends us on our way suitably prepared for Tryfan and the Glyders.

Trekking northwestward from the plateau we reach Bristly Ridge (4.6km), a point of divide between the two valleys; also a connecting link between the three magnificent peaks awaiting our attention. On the right (NE) is Bwlch Tryfan, offering southerly access to Tryfan summit from a point about 600ft below it.

Down from the ridge (NW) is Llyn Bochlwyd, a delightful mountain lake giving birth to Afon Nant Bochlwyd (5.6km), a stream of crystal brilliance. Then the descent to Ogwen (7.0km), grand junction of Eryri trackways.

host to mountains

Tryfan and the Glyders

Tryfan presents its toe to the A5 near the eastern end of Llyn Ogwen and offers its services to rock climbers on its western flank. An ascent via the northern ridge has the attraction of meeting the mountain in direct frontal challenge, accepting as reward an immediate expansion of view in more than one direction. The north ridge may be approached from a stile at the side of the A5, or from Gwern Gof Uchaf farmhouse (0.0km).

Tryfan displays superbly proportioned boulders, for the most part unfragmented, fairly clear of scree, with firm footholds for climbing. Yes, climbing. This mountain demands that walkers should become climbers. As a reward it presents a sculptured format, pleasing to all susceptibilities. Indeed, if Moses had been an inhabitant of Britain, he may well have chosen Tryfan on which to evolve the commandments. There would have also been a reasonable availability of shelter for forty days and nights. As for weather, he would have had to endure generally cooler and damper conditions than on Mount Sinai.

Being a complex mountain, Tryfan abounds in false summits though the subterfuge is not in the least displeasing; rather exuberantly one hopes for a continuum skyward. A contradictory urge impatiently seeks resolution. On reaching the peak (2.4km, 1½ml; elevation 917m, 3008ft) the climax becomes a revelation that sends the mind spinning in search of images.

Through capricious Snowdonia mists, vision alights upon a stage set. The decor is perfect. Any drama might be staged here from Shakespeare to contemporary fulminations on the state of the universe. Though in all candour one must admit that a play of plays most suitable for this exotic setting would be one depicting the romance of Eryri itself. Against a backdrop of cathedral majesty bestowed by those two massive pillars known as Adam and Eve, which may be glimpsed in transit along the valley floor, Snowdonia's great sweep of time might be most admirably distilled. Across the gap of

frozen profile

the upper Dyffryn Llygwy, almost within touching distance it seems, are those inimitable characters of the Carneddau with whom we are shortly to become better acquainted. It is likely they are waiting reticently beneath a steaming cap, guarding their secrets which presently we must induce them to reveal.

Departure means taking the inspiration. The bard reminds us:

viii.   Atgof a fydd y tecaf a feddi.
          Remembrance will be your finest possession.

Down, down to Bwlch Tryfan where lies the line of our peaks route from Pen-y-gwryd to Ogwen, and Bristly Ridge, host to an ascent of the Glyders.

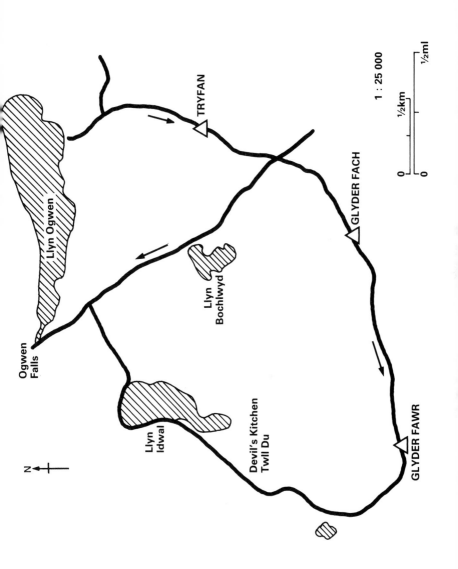

Llyn Ogwen

Ogwen
Falls

Llyn
Idwal

Devil's Kitchen
Twll Du

Llyn Bochlwyd

TRYFAN

GLYDER FACH

GLYDER FAWR

N

1 : 25 000

0   ½km

0   ½ml

Remembrance will be your finest possession? What does one's memorybank carry of this world above the three-thousand-foot level? The human factor: passing strangers automatically exchange greetings in a spirit of camaraderie. We are, after all, sharing an experience, though in our own private ways. Knowing the mind of another three-thousand-foot expeditioner is a near impossibility for we have a much-higher-than average inclination to guard our thoughts. The alternative, therefore, is to converse with an inner self. First, to Eryri's needs. All this tramping about in glorious rarified atmosphere: is there any danger that the mountains could be worn away? Of course. It has been happening on an increasing scale for decades and, possibly, this story may be a contribution to its increase. Just look at the depth of scree lying on the slopes. Is it fair to suggest that were the tramp of boots to cease instantly those screes would be colonised by plants, consolidated by soil, halting the insidious erosion that threatens to emasculate what we find exhilarating?

Plants. Evan Roberts, connoisseur of Eryri flora, discovered how plants told a story with a timescale extending back to the Ice Age. This terrain above three-thousand feet is their habitat. Of course, they should never be uprooted if found. But how might they be conserved and assisted to propagate that their invaluable story may be more precisely understood?

Eryri's needs suffer mental recession when confronted by examples of her sculpture. It lies all about Glyder Fach's summit massif. What happened during the Ice Age to produce such profusion? The peak itself (4.4km, 2¾ml; elevation 994m, 3262ft) must be the sharpest in Snowdonia. Certainly, when sitting on it there is a tendency to shift position in search of a more comfortable seat while taking care not to slide off the sculpture exhibits and between them into oblivion! Having come to terms with such hazards it is possible to appreciate the accommodation as a disorderly but well-lived-in abode where callers may drop in at any time taking the place as they find it.

Bwlch y Ddwy Glyder – the gap between the two Glyders – offers itself as a platform for photography, and at once a realisation dawns that perspective is everything. This is the place for justice to be done to the wide vista of the Nant Ffrancon Valley disappearing off the rim of the earth in some distant expanse of ocean. Pen yr Ole Wen, with its track route ascent onto the Carneddau, looks reasonably benign, as does the magnificent Tryfan. Clearly there is a need to avoid doing injustice to those commendable stalwarts. But what of lakeland? Ogwen might be an elongated serpent, listless and drowsy under a summer sun after devouring one of its own species. And the near lakes, Idwal and Bochlwyd? They could be siblings at extreme ends of a generation, each displaying its own shape and idiosyncracies. Certainly a pleasing contrast that may have been the subject of a deliberate design. Then we have the two Glyders themselves displaying such contrasting characters. To the east is Glyder Fach: flamboyant, disorganised, homely; a character whose pre-occupation would never preclude offering welcoming attentions to casual callers blowing in from anywhere. Glyder Fawr (6.3km, 3.94ml; elevation 999m, 3279ft) exudes a different mood. An austere patriarch harbouring some disappointment that the Ice Age should have swept almost all the intriguing features towards the eastern neighbour. However, there is recompense in residing above a feature with an expressive name like Twll Du – Devil's Kitchen.

Westward then northwestward over a scree slope that is being pressed downward into the cwm by pairs of passing boots. Somewhere beneath this overburden there must be solid mountain seeking vainly to stave off embarrassing exposure in the interests of its own integrity, that of the cwm and, indeed, of Llyn Idwal, the contraction of which is threatened under the weight of uninvited scree.

From the top of the Devil's Kitchen, magic descends with recollection that here a little white lily, Brwynddail y Mynydd – Lloydia Serotina – was re-discovered by Evan Roberts, the ex-quarryman, who became the first warden of Cwm Idwal nature reserve in 1954. Re-discovered because

Ice Age memorybank

the original discovery was made by Edward Lloyd, a naturalist of the late seventeenth century, after whom the plant was named. An Ice Age plant which was lost, it seems, for three centuries until Evan Roberts set out for a day's exploration in the Devil's Kitchen, its habitat.

Flora adapted to the Ice Age, performed life cycles beneath the frozen cap which in warmer climes melted and receded, leaving its offspring bereft. Mostly they died out, though a few specimens found tolerant limits acceptable in isolated Eryri retreats. Survivors recorded by Evan Roberts in *Llyfr Rhedyn Ei Daid* are:

Saxifraga oppositifolia (purple saxifrage)
Lloydia serotina (Snowdon lily, mountain spiderwort)
Dryas octopetala (eight petal 'oak')
Saxifraga cespitosa (tufted saxifrage)
Woodsia ilvensis (fern)
Polystichum lonchitis (holly fern)

Having descended the Devil's Kitchen (9.5km), and feeling disposed to contemplate by the shoreline of Llyn Idwal . . . suppose a windless summer evening when the sun is descending behind those monumental cliffs – this may be as close as one may come to pristine purity. The sound of water trickling faraway down a southern cliff. For the rest, silence. And pure water. Idwal is purity. The image will not be erased by recalling that the name derives from a prince of that name – the son of Owain Gwynedd, grandfather of Llywelyn the Great – who was brought here and drowned for reasons unknown. The event has relevance because this location was considered the remotest in Eryri where the deed could be most easily concealed.

When Eryri spares a golden evening, the bard's line is especially piquant here by Idwal.

Atgof a fydd y tecaf a feddi
Remembrance will be your finest possession

Carry it beyond the effort of departure; down the track with Tryfan having transmuted through a colour spectrum, now displaying herself in a rich mauve as if gowned for an evening performance at her summit theatre.

Ogwen

For thousands of years an Eryri pathway grand junction. From it gradients and distances are demanding. Rewards are tremendous. Surprise is guaranteed.

Llyn Ogwen gathers waters from the Carneddau, from the Glyders and Tryfan, tumbles over Ogwen Falls into Nant Ffrancon, becomes Afon Ogwen gliding down its wide valley through Bethesda which encapsulates quarrying in all its industrial and spiritual significance, sweeps past Penrhyn Castle to find communion with the Menai Strait.

The Carneddau Ridge

Pen Yr Ole Wen	2.2km	1.375ml
Carnedd Dafydd	4.4km	2¾ml
Carnedd Llywelyn	8.2km	5.1ml
Foel Grach	10.6km	6.6ml
Garnedd Uchaf	12.0km	7.5ml
Foel-fras	13.9km	8.7ml
Drum	16.5km	10.3ml
Carnedd y Ddelw	17.8km	11.1ml
Tal y Fan	22.8km	14.3ml
Conwy Mountain	32.0km	20.0ml
Conwy	35.2km	22.0ml

A few steps from the stile (0.0km) opposite Ogwen Falls is a world remote from the vehicle-bound one. Savour the design! A pre-historic convulsion built cliff faces and ramparts from where, on a windless day, the lake may be observed playing with an image of Tryfan. Catching Ogwen's mood is like grasping at a fleeting dream. She will allow a devotee but a brief indulgence. One of her favourite caprices is concealment beneath a cloak of mist through which she might reveal a mere glimpse of her western lips and white pearls cascading down her slender neck. Beyond the lower cliffs one must reconcile to loss of intimacy: up ahead is a steep south-facing bank.

It is clothed in heathers playing host to wasps which are apt to react angrily to sudden intrusion. Among the heathers is a small-leafed plant that produces a delicious berry with a multiplicity of names. In Welsh it is *llus*. In English it has a string of names: blaeberry, bilberry, blueberry, whortleberry, whinberry. It is usually described in English Welsh as *whinberry*. In the ripening season a climber's reward can be a tart-tasting breakfast and fingers stained dark red. Recollection of other Eryri locations brings visions of whinberry jam, tarts, pies – all absolutely delicious. The plants colonise unpolluted south-facing slopes which offer some sunshine, usually among rocks providing shelter. Once available in profusion, it is now a rare delight to encounter this delectable little black berry.

Yr Ole Wen – The White Light? When the ancients chose names did they see a white bank, brilliantly lit at the head of Nant Ffrancon? Pen yr Ole Wen – Top of the (brilliant) White Light? The altitude at Ogwen is 1000ft. Pen yr Ole Wen (2.2km, 1.375ml; elevation 979m, 3211ft). The climb: 2211 feet in 1.375 miles.

A world upon which the sea bestows its inimitable fragrance. Fill the lungs with its purity conveyed through high level filtration directly from the ocean. In slight inebriation one blinks westward, northward, eastward. This peak is sometimes bypassed by climbers in a hurry to skirt round the rim of the cwm. Pity, their loss. Down below is *Ffynnon Loer* – well of the moon. In this state of intoxication, belief is credible. The well of the moon issues its crystal waters upon Ogwen whose ambience seems now like a distant world deep in the past.

After constrictions of the climb there is an urge to run from Pen yr Ole Wen along the top of Cwm Lloer. Above moon landscape, the features of which the original namers recognised long ago before notions of space rockets, running is an expression of freedom.

Northward, northeastward. Trainers for marathons may run and run!

Carnedd Dafydd (4.4km, 2¾ml; elevation 1044m, 3423ft) sits atop a confluence of cwms – to southeast, northwest, northeast – listening immutably to their wails. Much the strongest complaint arrives from over the clifftop northeast, generated by whiplashes around precipitous crags piled with dizzying imbalance one upon another, then hurled agonisingly skywards where clouds skurry in haste from its demented roar.

This is the music of Ysgolion Duon – black ladders – and we are on *Cefn Ysgolion Duon* – the back of black ladders. Dare look down into the cauldron and a vicious spitting slaps the face. Turn the back to the cefn. Back to back. The well of the moon is peaceful. Further out eastward is a limitless space in which sight and mind rest beyond horizons. Exhilaration breeds illusion that anything is possible, the world is limitless, one may simply do to achieve. A frantic mist rushing up the black ladders clutches at escaping clouds seeking sanctity above the valleys. Mist concentrates the mind upon compass bearings: eastward veering slowly to northeastward. The route lies along a ridge that falls away sharply to either side. That settled, if mist excludes views the mind may concentrate elsewhere, such as on the joys of walking alone or with a companion.

Who seeks solitude on mountains? Moses, for one. Could the commandments have endured more than two millennia if he had been in company? Company going about such matters is a committee. A committee might have submitted a minority report. How might civilisation have coped with an alternative list of commandments?

Eastward, southeastward, is a rectangular wedge of grey-blue-green locked into the upper end of Cwm Llugwy, the expanse immediately right. *Llugwy Ffynnon* – the well of the Llygwy – shares a distinction with other lakes worldwide in giving birth to a famous river. What is so famous about the Afon Llugwy? Its volume, or length, would not, of course, compare with say, that of the Nile; though it could claim a contribution to civilisation.

Not in the manner of High Street, Betws-y-coed, in its present mode. Rather to Betws as a source of inspiration to artists. In that role Betws may claim immortality. Although there is a confluence of three rivers at Betws-y-coed, the design of romantic scenery is, essentially, that of the Llugwy. Most renowned of those who sought inspiration in its beauties was David Cox (1783–1859).

David Cox spent many summers painting at Betws-y-coed, working with a concept that sublime ideas could be expressed through subjects like mountains, cottages, water

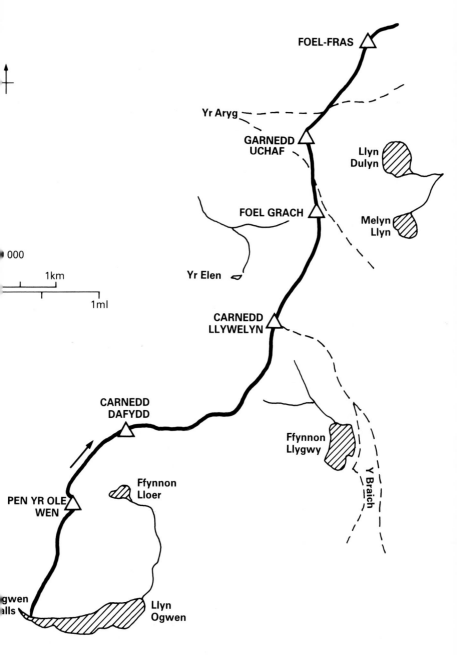

FOEL-FRAS

Yr Aryg

GARNEDD
UCHAF

Llyn
Dulyn

FOEL GRACH

Melyn
Llyn

Yr Elen

CARNEDD
LLYWELYN

CARNEDD
DAFYDD

Ffynnon
Llygwy

Y Braich

Ffynnon
Lloer

PEN YR OLE
WEN

gwen
alls

Llyn
Ogwen

000

1km

1ml

79

mills, meadows, river valleys. These capricious skies with which Snowdonia projects her moods he was able to capture with heightened drama on canvas as if portending cataclysm. His canvas mountains, inspired by Eryri, impress a message that leaves one appreciating real mountains better. The people in his landscapes are unobtrusive, all being representative of the scene, expressing a harmony between humans and nature. The Llugwy, its surroundings, its people, were captured in art, as was the Royal Oak Inn, David Cox's lodgings, which became the rendezvous for an international artists' set.

On the eastern side of Ffynnon Llugwy two paths bearing N/S may be distinguished, one near to the shore of the lake, the other lying along *Y Braich* – The Arm – well named as a branch ridge of the Carneddau. The two paths originate from different points in the Llugwy Valley, converge north of Ffynnon Llugwy on Y Braich which joins the main trunk of the mountain chain at Carnedd Llywelyn, Eryri's second highest peak (8.2km, 5.1ml; elevation 1064m, 3485ft).

A battered summit, 75 feet lower than Snowdon, and on that account enjoying the distinction of having all its visitors arrive on foot, all the sitters on the cairn having sacrificed sweat and effort in order to pay homage to a peak with a distinguished name. So, do we gather in anticipation of camaraderie? Come on, no need for solitary contemplation now. Animation flows most freely from those whose mother tongue is not English. Does this say something about national character? Or, that those visiting a foreign country feel freer to ask questions? Interest centres on location of the peak Yr Elen. From where we are sitting it is north-westward, 300°, about 2km, at the end of the western ridge supporting Llywelyn and 333 feet lower. The two mountains sit in tandem, keeping guard over a small lake at their feet where Eryri's wild mares come to foal. Interest burgeons! A German speaker declares that the wild ponies of Eryri are fantastic, more a symbol of freedom than the wild goats of Austria. Sight of the wild ponies stirs the mind to wonder. The entire area of the mountains is theirs to roam. They enjoy a kind of tranquil freedom that produces a self-assured dignity. And then, in spring, some imprinted ancestral memory induces a pregnant mare along an ancient route. She makes her way to the secret cwm – Cwm Caseg, the mare's cwm – and to the private lake – *Ffynnon Caseg,* the mare's well – beneath the shelter of Llywelyn and Yr Elen. Her foal is born and she tends it, in company with other mares and their foals.

Departure is a drifting away. Piecemeal dispersion. Northwestward to Yr Elen above the mare's well. Northeastward along the ridge.

The ridge, a plane in the sky, leads a life of its own, untroubled by the nether world, in communion only with the sea and sky. The sea is remote but always present, allowing a brilliant view westward and northward to itself when its mood is benign, projecting an opaque sky if disturbed, producing the kind of effect that inspired David Cox in his painting.

A rock outcrop grows and grows into a primitive castle with ramparts and battlements. In its shelter is a Refuge Hut. Below Foel Grach peak (10.6km, 6.6ml; elevation 974m, 3196ft), eastwards, are two lakes, Dulyn and Melynllyn, sunk in huge rock potholes. Further out is a long finger of water, Llyn Eigiau, pointing northward against east-facing precipitous cliffs. All three are engaged in supplying Carneddau rain to a distant world whose relevance, at this elevation, seems questionable.

Above the lakes an old packhorse trail which began its circuitous route way down in Tal-y-bont, mounts the contours, lies parallel with the ridge for a few hundred metres, then joins it (11.4km), and continues nothwestward to merge with another trail west of the peak Yr Aryg. Due westward at 11.4km, a ridge slopes away giving birth to Afon Wen – pure river – yes, pure, which by recollection of climbing the ridge on a warm day and drinking its water, must rate as an understatement. It joins the Afon Caseg whose inspiration is the mare's lake at the feet of Llywelyn and Yr Elen, gathers strength in the long valley above Gerlan, flows down through Bethesda to merge with the Afon Ogwen below Nant Ffrancon.

Garnedd Uchaf – the Upper Garnedd (12.0km, 7.5ml; elevation 915m, 3000ft) – might be a battlefield ruin, wearing a self-effacing air on account of it occupying a slight depression in the ridge's majestic flow. Veer northeastward, and after 500m meet another packhorse trail, the direct route from Tal-y-bont and Llanbedr-y-cennin to Bangor. This was the chosen route of those packhorsemen who were not obliged to make calls at cottages to the south of Eigiau. Now an exhilarating walking route, the old trail has left its hollowed impression, though not on the ridge itself. After 150 years or thereabout, nature has managed a fair amount of elimination. Beyond Yr Aryg the two trails merge, providing a pleasant descent to Llandegai.

At Foel-fras (13.9km, 8.7ml; elevation 942m, 3091ft), the mind must begin to adjust to departure from this rarefied world. A feeling of moorland is confirmed by a certain cry and sight of a long slender curved bill.

ix.   Dy alwad glywir hanner dydd
     Fel ffliwt hyfrydlais uwch y rhos.

     Your call can be heard at midday
     Like a sonorous flute above the moor.

Sounds carry and are amplified on the moor. The curlew's call may be heard far off as it flies away from intruders, its sound at last mixing with others; human sounds; voices. Bodies appear through the mist like ghosts, preying upon susceptibilities, becoming solid for a moment, then drifting away into fantasy.

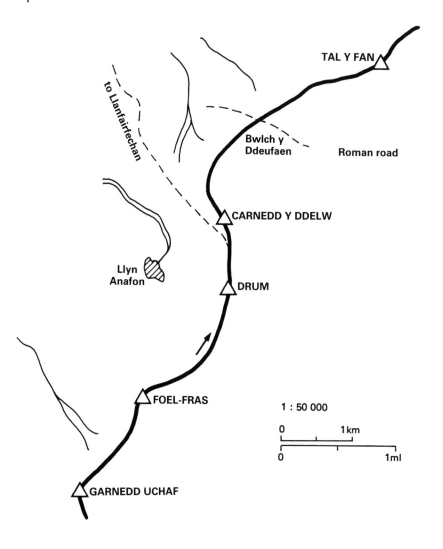

N

TAL Y FAN

Bwlch y
Ddeufaen

Roman road

to Llanfairfechan

CARNEDD Y DDELW

Llyn
Anafon

DRUM

FOEL-FRAS

1 : 50 000

0   1 km

0   1 ml

GARNEDD UCHAF

The purposeful sound of distant water – relentless, inexhaustible, everlasting – penetrates to the ridge. Afon Goch flows northwestward from the Carneddau, gathering volume exponentially in a headlong rush towards *Rhaeadr-fawr* – big falls – and a drop of 70m (225ft) to the valley floor while draping the cliff face with a swaying white curtain. The sound of the big falls above Aber is supplemented by Rhaeadr-bach a short distance southwestward. Rhaedr-bach's river joins its larger neighbour below the falls to become Afon Rhaeadr-fawr which is joined from the next valley by Afon Anafon whose cacophony is like the eternal working of the sea, suggesting transition from a sweeping Atlantic gale to a measured breeze of the strait, from harsh summit rigour to soft pastel shades of gorse and heather; and mellow hills silhouetted on a seascape that may be emerald or turquoise, blue or grey, depending upon infinite permutations of mood.

Drum, or Carnedd Penydorth-goch (16.5km, 10.3ml; elevation 771m, 2529ft), is a parting of ways. Topographically, the inclination is northwestward down the beaten track, across the Roman road and onto green paths through gorsed and heathered slopes, to Llanfairfechan. That could be one ending to the story. Resisting it in anticipation of other exhilarations, one adheres to a fence line northward to Carnedd y Ddelw (17.8km, 11.1ml; elevation 686m, 2250ft) sitting atop the declining ridge concealing another which, 500m further on, slopes away northeastward – 040° to 050°. Down the slope 800m we join company with a dry stone wall, guiding descent into the valley while offering itself for evaluation.

It began as raw materials freely available on or near the construction site, requiring no mortar or other binding material. Once the stones were interlocked and counterbalanced, its life extended to infinity, withstanding almost any vicissitude, virtually maintenance free, completely harmonised with the environment. Comparison with any other form of boundary marking leaves the dry stone wall unchallengeably pre-eminent. An admirer wonders at the manual effort required to effect a construction on a moun-

white power

85

tainside and reflects that were such a project undertaken today, mechanical aids could render most of the back-breaking labour superfluous.

Bwlch y Ddeufaen – Pass of Two Stones. On the descent, they can be seen beyond the wall on the right. The nearer upright stone is 2m high and the other, about 80m distant, stands 3m high. Pre-historic, though of uncertain date and purpose, part of their function must have been as markers for transit through the pass. The trackway was used by the conquering Romans, under their governor, Julius Agricola, from about 78 A.D. However, the Roman army's need was for an engineered construction.

The Romans designed and built a road for wheeled transport, about 15 feet wide, appearing as a shelf or raised bank according to the terrain. In a brief timespan of less than two millennia, nature has obscured or consumed most of their effort. But in Bwlch y Ddeufaen there is established archeological evidence. The road's general line is shown to lie between these points recorded as map references: 74237183, about 200m east of the Maen-y-Bardd pre-historic tomb, westward to 72687135, to 68907263, which crosses this route at the bottom of the pass (20.2km, 12.6ml).

If, standing on or near the line of the road the evidence is not immediately apparent, consider its timespan. The road could have been in regular use as an arterial link between Caerhun in the Conwy Valley and Segontium by the Menai Strait for something like 300 years: an equivalence between our own time and that of the Glorious Revolution, the climax of the seventeenth-century struggle in Britain between absolute monarchy and parliamentary government, settled finally in 1688, which prepared the world for the way it is today.

Tal y Fan presents its southwestern foot for ascent (070°) in alignment with the dry stone wall, veering to 030° and N to a wall corner (21.0km), then eastward. This long bulky mountain possesses two summits of almost equivalent height and from the lower (21.4km, 13.4ml; elevation 598m, 1963ft), the sea impresses its immediate presence. How fortunate if it paints one of its exquisite late afternoon pictures:

still air under cloud mountains tinged with shades of turquoise.

x.   A gwyrdd fôr yn gorwedd fel
Gwridog aur hyd y gorwel,
'Roedd dydd ar ei ddedwyddaf,
A blwyddyn yn nherfyn haf.
A gwrid yr hwyr ar gread yr awron
Yn rhoi gemliw grug ym mhlyg yr eigion.

And the blue sea lying like
Shining gold on the horizon,
The day at its most mellow,
The year brimming with summer.
The blush of evening on time's creation
Planting jewelled heather in folds of ocean.

Hope is sustained that the sea's gift will not be withdrawn while one is in a hollow or behind a crag. Steadily down and then expectantly up round the summit knoll to the peak (22.8km, 14.3ml; elevation 610m, 2000ft).

A further 500m (065°) along to the edge of the summit massif, there is a viewing platform for appreciating a creative sea in artistic mood. In the distance a golden elevation plucks into the sky. The bearing is 030° and all between is freedom within that commanding constraint. Freedom of the mountains still; shared freedom with the ponies, foals still trailing the mares, looking with casual curiosity at a creature striding away downhill across the expanse.

A ridge walker's instinct is for high ground and the opportunities it allows. Paths across the ridge are ever tempting, seeking to distract downward into some cosy valley with blind ends. Resolve is tested against determination to reach a peak by the sea, a peak which holds a promise that only the sea can fulfil.

The Afon Gyrach flows from the moor into a narrow valley clothed in pleasant woodland: down, down to the entrancing Capelulo at the western end of Sychnant Pass. Running along an upper contour above Capelulo, there is temptation to reach out in salute of Allt Wen – White Hill. A commanding bastion, and for thousands of years the key to possession of the Pass. Against a backcloth of immense sky the power of the fort implanted on its top seems undiminished, able to detain instantly any movement in the narrow valley below.

The contour of the hill leads to the choke point in the Pass (30km, 18¾ml).

Northward to Allt Wen's eastern foot, then northeastward and eastward to the sea and its great expanse of bay. And its secret. The secret that Conwy Bay has kept, nurtured, and revealed to its friends. The secret that is the source of bardic inspiration, and of musical composition. The legend that seems so true.

Below Conwy peak (32km, 20ml; elevation 247m, 810ft) is *Llys Helig* – the Court of Helig. Not visible, of course, because it is under the sea.

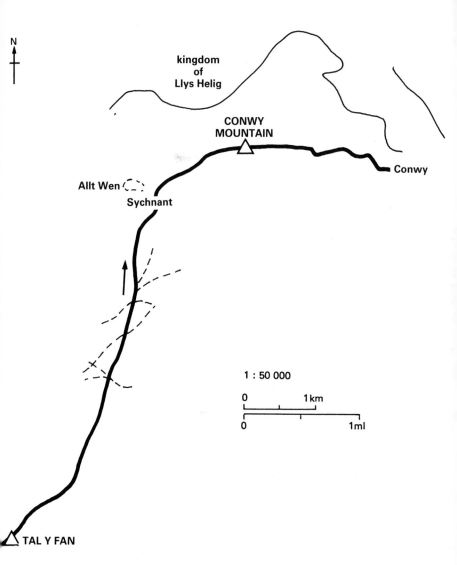

xi. There was a kingdom – close to the shore,
     And there were people – five hundred, or more,
     Opulent, subservient, dissident, and well content.

     And there were riches – silver and gold,
     Diamonds and rubies – more than you could hold,
     Beautiful, wonderful, plentiful, bountiful.

That the legend should have endured some 1400 years, including a recent resurgence, may be due to a classical quality of theme. Helig, chieftain, lord or king over an area now beneath Conwy Bay, had a beautiful daughter, Gwendyd, for whom he wished to arrange an eminent marriage. Gwendyd, however, was in love with a commoner, a servant named Tathal. (Gwendyd and Tathal are the names assigned to the couple in a musical drama, The Circle of Gilt – included in which is the lyric above – staged in 1982 at Aberconwy School) Opportunity for Tathal arrived in the form of a nobleman out walking alone and wearing a golden neck wreath, or torque, an emblem of social rank. Tathal attacked the nobleman, killed him, put on the golden torque, presented himself to Gwendyd who told him to bury the body so it could never be found. While digging the grave Tathal heard a voice saying "Dial a ddaw, dial a ddaw – revenge will come, revenge will come." In terror he fled to Gwendyd who told him to return to the grave and ask the voice when revenge would come. In doing so, Tathal was told: "In the time of your children, your grandchildren, your great grandchildren." Gwendyd was relieved. "No need to worry, Tathal," she said. "We'll be dead by then." Which proved a false prophesy.

Gwendyd and Tathal were married. One evening a great feast was in progress at Llys Helig. The bard, Cynan, sets the scene:

xii.   Difyr, difyr oedd bwrdd y wledd,
A Helig ap Glanawg yn yfed mewn hedd
Yn ei gaer yn sŵn y môr.

"Yfwch i heddwch fy henaint teg!
Ac yfwch i'r Iseldiroedd chweg,
A'r mur sydd rhyngddynt a'r môr!"

Pleasant, pleasant was the table of the feast,
And Helig ap Glanawg drinking in peace
In his fort within sound of the sea.

"Drink to the peace of my old age!
And drink to the pleasant lowlands,
And the wall between them and the sea!"

In the early hours a maid was sent to the cellar for
mead. She returned with a message of foreboding.

"Mae Pysgod yn nofio yn seler y medd."
"Fish are swimming in the mead cellar."

Helig knew that revenge had come.

"Ffo allan, fy merch, a'm mantell a'm cledd.
Ffo, ffo o gyrraedd y mor!

"Cyrch, fy merch, tua'r Penmaen Mawr,
Daeth dial yr Arglwydd Ior.
Nac edrych yn ol hyd doriad gwawr,
Gwrando gynddaredd y mor!"

"Escape out, my girl, with my mantle and sword,
Escape, escape from reach of the sea!

"Go, my girl, towards Penmaen Mawr,
The revenge of God has come.
Don't look back until break of day,
Listen to the rage of the sea!"

These events are alleged to have occurred in the half century between 532 and 582 AD. One can swim by the walls of Llys Helig, it is claimed, round a tower, in company with conger eels. The shoreline of the old kingdom is the present five-fathom line. Within two miles of the present shoreline is a petrified forest, and beneath six or eight inches of Lafan sand is about two yards of peat bog containing remains of oak, beech, hazel and collections of their nuts in safe keeping away from atmospheric destruction.

A detached opinion about Llys Helig proposes that an earthquake occurred early one morning in the mid-sixth century, resulting in a lowering of the sea bed and creation of broad expanse of bay that we can enjoy on the descent to Conwy (35.2km, 22ml).

frontier fortress

Bards' Roll

i. **Llyn y Gadair**   T.H. Parry-Williams

ii. **Bugeiles yr Wyddfa**   Eos Bradwen

iii. **Bannau Gwynion**   R. Williams Parry

iv. **Wild Honey**   M Frayn

v.

vi.

vii.

viii.   **Yr Haf a Cherddi Eraill**   R. Williams Parry

ix.

x.

xi. **The Circle of Gilt**   T. Biggin and R. Grindley

xii. **Balad Llys Helig**   Cynan

Picture Locations

Focus Publications
9 Priors Road
Windsor
Berks SL4 4PD.

Bibliography

Williams Parry, R., *Yr Haf a Cherddi Eraill*, Gwasg y Bala, 1956.

Emrys Parry, T., *Barddoniaeth Robert Williams Parry, Astudiaeth Feirniadol*, Gwasg Gee.

Y Flodeugerdd Gymraeg (W.J. Gruffydd, editor), Gwasg Prifysgol, Cymru, Caerdydd, 1940.

Cerddi Cynan y Casgliad Cyflawn, Gwasg y Brython, Lerpwl, 1967.

Gruffydd, D., Gwyndaf, R., *Llyfr Rhedyn ei Daid: Portread o Evan Roberts, Capel Curig, Llysieuwr,* Gwasg Dwyfor, 1987.

Frayn, M., *Anton Chekhov, Wild Honey,* Methuen, 1984.

Bradley, A.G., *Owen Glyndwr and the last Struggle for Welsh Independence,* Putnam, London, 1902.

Winson, J., *The Little Wonder,* Ffestiniog Railway Company and Michael Joseph, 1975.

Nash-Williams, V.E., Jarret, M.G., *The Roman Frontier in Wales.* University of Wales Press, Cardiff, 1969.

Jones, A., *A History of Gruffydd ap Cynan,* University of Manchester Press, 1910.

HMSO, *An Inventory of Ancient Monuments in Caernarvonshire, Volume II,* 1960.

Biggin T., Grindley, R., *The Circle of Gilt,* Conwy, 1982.

Ordnance Survey Publications